Perfect KS3 English practice — from CGP!

This fantastic CGP book is full of 10-Minute Workouts — just the thing you need for quick, regular English practice throughout Year 8.

Every workout covers Reading, Writing and SPaG skills, with a variety of texts to put you to the test. Plus, there's one for each week of the school year — incredible!

Answers are included at the back, along with a handy score sheet to track your progress throughout the year. You can thank us later!

A note for teachers, parents and caregivers

Just something to bear in mind if you're choosing further reading for Year 8 pupils — all the extracts in this book are suitable for children of this age, but we can't vouch for the full texts they're taken from, or other works by the same authors.

L.M. Montgomery is a trademark of Heirs of L.M. Montgomery Inc.

Published by CGP
ISBN: 978 1 83774 049 9

Editors: Robbie Driscoll, Rebecca Greaves, Nathan Mair, Ilana Pearce, Kirsty Sweetman

With thanks to Emma Cleasby and John Sanders for the proofreading.

With thanks to Jade Sim for the copyright research.

Clipart from Corel®

Printed by W & G Baird Ltd, Antrim.
Based on the classic CGP style created by Richard Parsons.

Text, design, layout and original illustrations
© Coordination Group Publications Ltd. (CGP) 2023
All rights reserved.

Photocopying this book is not permitted, even if you have a CLA licence.
Extra copies are available from CGP with next day delivery • 0800 1712 712 • www.cgpbooks.co.uk

How to Use this Book

- This book contains 36 workouts. We've split them into 3 sections — one for each term, with 12 workouts each. There's roughly one workout for every week of the school year.

- Each workout is out of 12 marks and should take about 10 minutes to complete.

- The workouts start with a short warm-up question, followed by a text with some reading questions. Pupils then move on to a spelling, punctuation or grammar question and finish with some writing skills practice.

- The workouts progress in difficulty, so they're perfect for ensuring that pupils are getting to grips with Year 8 English.

- Answers, a glossary and a score sheet can be found at the back of the book.

The contents page for each term shows you the main reading and writing skills and text types covered in each workout.

Some of these topics are then retested in the following terms at a slightly higher level to provide more practice.

Each workout also tests a different spelling, punctuation or grammar skill, providing practice of a range of topics across the book.

The workouts in each term can be done in any order — pick the one that best suits the needs of your pupils.

The tick boxes on the contents pages can help you to keep a record of which workouts have been attempted.

Contents — Autumn Term

- ☑ **Workout 1** 2
  - Reading Non-Fiction: Identifying Types of Text
  - Writing Non-Fiction: Planning
- ☑ **Workout 2** 4
  - Reading Non-Fiction: Finding Evidence in the Text
  - Writing Non-Fiction: Planning
- ☑ **Workout 3** 6
  - Reading Poetry: Structure
  - Writing Poetry: Haikus
- ☑ **Workout 4** 8
  - Reading Fiction: What You Think
  - Writing Fiction: Mood and Character
- ☑ **Workout 5** 10
  - Reading Non-Fiction: Tone
  - Writing Non-Fiction: Writing to Persuade and Argue
- ☑ **Workout 6** 12
  - Reading Poetry: Working Out What's Going On
  - Writing Poetry: Rhythm and Descriptive Language
- ☑ **Workout 7** 14
  - Reading Drama: Working Out What's Going On
  - Writing Drama: Play Scripts
- ☑ **Workout 8** 16
  - Reading Non-Fiction: Audience
  - Writing Non-Fiction: Writing to Persuade
- ☑ **Workout 9** 18
  - Reading Fiction: Summarising
  - Writing Fiction: Structure
- ☑ **Workout 10** 20
  - Reading Non-Fiction: Purpose
  - Writing Non-Fiction: Essays
- ☑ **Workout 11** 22
  - Reading Poetry: Working Out What's Going On
  - Writing Poetry: Rhythm
- ☑ **Workout 12** 24
  - Reading Fiction: Language Techniques
  - Writing Fiction: Figurative Language

Contents — Autumn Term

- [ ] **Workout 1** 2
  - Reading Non-Fiction: Identifying Types of Text
  - Writing Non-Fiction: Planning
- [ ] **Workout 2** 4
  - Reading Non-Fiction: Finding Evidence in the Text
  - Writing Non-Fiction: Planning
- [ ] **Workout 3** 6
  - Reading Poetry: Structure
  - Writing Poetry: Haikus
- [ ] **Workout 4** 8
  - Reading Fiction: What You Think
  - Writing Fiction: Mood and Character
- [ ] **Workout 5** 10
  - Reading Non-Fiction: Tone
  - Writing Non-Fiction: Writing to Persuade and Argue
- [ ] **Workout 6** 12
  - Reading Poetry: Working Out What's Going On
  - Writing Poetry: Rhythm and Descriptive Language
- [ ] **Workout 7** 14
  - Reading Drama: Working Out What's Going On
  - Writing Drama: Play Scripts
- [ ] **Workout 8** 16
  - Reading Non-Fiction: Audience
  - Writing Non-Fiction: Writing to Persuade
- [ ] **Workout 9** 18
  - Reading Fiction: Summarising
  - Writing Fiction: Structure
- [ ] **Workout 10** 20
  - Reading Non-Fiction: Purpose
  - Writing Non-Fiction: Essays
- [ ] **Workout 11** 22
  - Reading Poetry: Working Out What's Going On
  - Writing Poetry: Rhythm
- [ ] **Workout 12** 24
  - Reading Fiction: Language Techniques
  - Writing Fiction: Figurative Language

Contents — Spring Term

☑ **Workout 1** 26
  - Reading Non-Fiction: Layout and Structure
  - Writing Non-Fiction: Quoting

☑ **Workout 2** 28
  - Reading Fiction: Understanding Characters
  - Writing Fiction: Building Character

☑ **Workout 3** 30
  - Reading Non-Fiction: Summarising
  - Writing Non-Fiction: Redrafting and Proofreading

☑ **Workout 4** 32
  - Reading Poetry: Themes
  - Writing Poetry: Rhyming Couplets

☑ **Workout 5** 34
  - Reading Fiction: Understanding Setting
  - Writing Fiction: Building Setting

☑ **Workout 6** 36
  - Reading Non-Fiction: Working Out What's Going On
  - Writing Non-Fiction: Writing to Inform, Explain and Advise

☑ **Workout 7** 38
  - Reading Fiction: Language Techniques
  - Writing Fiction: Redrafting and Proofreading

☑ **Workout 8** 40
  - Reading Non-Fiction: Language Techniques
  - Writing Non-Fiction: Essays

☑ **Workout 9** 42
  - Reading Poetry: Voice
  - Writing Poetry: Grammar

☑ **Workout 10** 44
  - Reading Fiction: Structure
  - Writing Fiction: Redrafting and Proofreading

☑ **Workout 11** 46
  - Reading Non-Fiction: Comparing Texts
  - Writing Non-Fiction: Writing to Persuade and Argue

☑ **Workout 12** 48
  - Reading Drama: Interpreting Plays
  - Writing Drama: Quoting

Contents — Summer Term

☑ **Workout 1** 50
- Reading Non-Fiction: What You Think
- Writing Non-Fiction: Formal and Informal Language

☑ **Workout 2** 52
- Reading Poetry: Techniques
- Writing Poetry: Language Techniques

☑ **Workout 3** 54
- Reading Fiction: Context
- Writing Fiction: Descriptive Language

☑ **Workout 4** 56
- Reading Non-Fiction: Layout and Structure
- Writing Non-Fiction: Structure

☑ **Workout 5** 58
- Reading Fiction: Themes
- Writing Fiction: Writing Stories

☑ **Workout 6** 60
- Reading Non-Fiction: Author's Intentions
- Writing Non-Fiction: Writing to Inform, Explain and Advise

☑ **Workout 7** 62
- Reading Poetry: Structure
- Writing Poetry: Language Techniques

☑ **Workout 8** 64
- Reading Drama: Staging and Performance
- Writing Drama: Play Scripts

☑ **Workout 9** 66
- Reading Non-Fiction: Language Techniques
- Writing Non-Fiction: Redrafting and Proofreading

☑ **Workout 10** 68
- Reading Fiction: Comparing Texts
- Writing Fiction: Setting and Atmosphere

☑ **Workout 11** 70
- Reading Non-Fiction: Tone and Audience
- Writing Non-Fiction: Essays

☑ **Workout 12** 72
- Reading Poetry: Techniques
- Writing Poetry: Mood

Answers 74

Glossary & Score Sheet 83

Autumn Term: Workout 1

Warm up

1. Which of the following is **not** a type of non-fiction text? Circle the correct option.

   | a leaflet | an autobiography | a mystery novel | a newspaper article |

   (1 mark)

Reading Questions

A First-aid plasters were invented by Earle Dickson in 1920, when he created one for his accident-prone wife. Though not an instant hit, plasters were being mass-produced by 1924, and in the 40s, during WWII, millions were sent to soldiers to keep in their medical kits.

B The trolley scooter is the finest invention of the year, and it's coming to a SwiftShop supermarket near you! Scooter your trolley around the aisles and you could cut the time spent on your weekly shop in half. It's the best mode of supermarket transport out there!

2. a) What type of text do you think each extract above is from?

   Text A .... Text B ....

   b) Explain your answer for Text B. Refer to two techniques in your answer.

   ....

   ....

   (2 marks)

3. a) Write down a fact from one of the texts.

   ....

   b) Write down an opinion from one of the texts.

   ....

   (2 marks)

Spelling, Punctuation & Grammar Question

4. Fill in the gap in each sentence using 'There', 'They're' or 'Their'.

   a) .... newest invention is the flying car.

   b) .... calling it the best thing since sliced bread.

   c) .... may well be flying carpets soon too.

   (3 marks)

Writing Questions

5. Read this short plan for a news article. Rewrite the final bullet point to improve it.

   > - Akeem, an eccentric scientist, claims he has invented a time machine.
   > - He says he travelled back to Pompeii in AD 79 to see Mount Vesuvius.
   > - He gave our newspaper an interesting quote about it.

   ....

   ....
   (1 mark)

6. Plan the first three points of a speech based on one of the prompts below.

   | Why is it important to invest money into researching cures for diseases? | Are physical copies of books still necessary now that eReaders exist? |

   Point 1 ....

   ....

   Point 2 ....

   ....

   Point 3 ....

   ....
   (3 marks)

Score: / 12

Autumn Term: Workout 2

> **Warm up**
>
> 1. Tick the correct option. Making an inference means to draw a conclusion ....
>
>   based on no evidence ☐   based on opinions ☐   based on evidence ☐
>
>   *(1 mark)*

Reading Questions

JACKPOT LOTTERY TICKET FOUND IN BIRD'S NEST

A birdwatcher has won big this week after discovering a winning lottery ticket in a robin's nest in Redbreast Park.

Local birdwatcher, Wren Warbler, had been observing the robin's behaviour through her binoculars when she registered that it was using a somewhat unconventional material to help build its nest.

Warbler initially paid no notice to the ticket, thinking it the remains of an unlucky loss. However, what appeared to be trash was actually treasure, which Warbler soon found out when her partner, Sophie, insisted she check the ticket's numbers online.

The couple donated a large sum of the money to the Bird Conservation Trust, adding that the eyes of the Trust's founder lit up at the act of generosity. The couple plan to spend the rest of their winnings birdwatching abroad.

2. How can you tell that the ticket was of great value?

   ....
   (1 mark)

3. a) Which word best describes how Wren felt when she first saw the ticket?

   shocked ☐   thrilled ☐   indifferent ☐

   b) Write out the part of the text that tells you this.

   ....
   (1 mark)

4. How can you tell that the couple's donation to the Trust was appreciated?

   ....
   (1 mark)

Spelling, Punctuation & Grammar Question

5. Underline the word in each sentence that is missing a possessive apostrophe. Then write the word correctly above the incorrect word.

   a) Many species of birds are at risk due to climate changes impact on the world.

   b) A study was done by Wrens colleagues about which owls face the most threats.

   c) The studys results show snowy owls will suffer from changes to their habitat.

   (3 marks)

Writing Question

6. Imagine your local council is planning to cut down a forest that is home to a vulnerable species of bird. Using the table below, plan a letter to the council outlining why they should cancel this plan.

Introduction	....
Point 1	....
Point 2	....
Point 3	....
Conclusion	....

(5 marks)

Score: /12

Autumn Term: Workout 3

Warm up

1. What is meant by the 'rhythm' of a poem?

   ....

   (1 mark)

Reading Questions

> In floats a quiet breeze,
> Gentle waves, restful trees,
> Calm, serenity and peace.
>
> Then flares of lightning strike the sky.
>
> Now spindly tree limbs are flailing
> And frenzied sirens are wailing
> And whole power grids are failing
>
> And fishermen's boats aren't sailing
> And fierce gales are prevailing
> This storm's power is unfailing
>
> Then tired winds sit still.
>
> In floats a quiet breeze,
> Gentle waves, restful trees,
> Calm, serenity and peace.

2. Tick a box to show whether each sentence is true or false.

                                               True   False

   a) The poem's rhythm changes between stanzas. ☐ ☐

   b) The second and fifth stanzas act as turning points. ☐ ☐

   (2 marks)

3. The third and fourth stanzas don't use much punctuation. What is the effect of this?

   ....

   ....

   (1 mark)

4. Why do you think the first stanza is repeated at the end? What is the effect of this?

   ....

   ....

   (2 marks)

Spelling, Punctuation & Grammar Question

5. Fill in the gaps in the poem using the words in the box.
Only use each word once.

| though | through | thorough |

I trudged home alone .... the storm,

.... I didn't feel too forlorn.

To my house I retired,

Where my roaring fire,

Did a .... job of keeping me warm.

(3 marks)

Writing Question

6. The poem below is a haiku. A haiku is made up of three lines, with 5 syllables in the first line, 7 syllables in the second line, and 5 syllables in the third line.

> Darkness is brewing
> Charcoal clouds loom over us
> We brace for impact.

Haikus don't need to rhyme.

Write your own haiku about another type of weather.
Use the correct number of syllables in each line.

....

....

....

(3 marks)

Score: /12

Autumn Term: Workout 4

Warm up

1. What is meant by the 'mood' of a text?

   ....
   (1 mark)

Reading Questions

> As I peer through the gap in the curtains, my face is illuminated by the stage lights darting back and forth, taunting me. "Come out, come out, wherever you are..."
>
> Then there are the other voices. My last director saying I'm not "up to scratch". My parents suggesting I "find a more stable career". The devil perching on my shoulder, smiling wickedly, saying, "You can't do it. Spare us all the bother and go home."
>
> Everything up until this moment has gone wrong, so if you do the maths, this performance will follow suit. The voices will get louder, and multiply, and become so deafening that I'll lose myself in them, and my dreams of stardom will end in disaster.
>
> "But then again," a new voice whispers, "what if this time things go right?"

2. Using your own words, describe the mood created in the first paragraph.

   ....
   (1 mark)

3. What effect does the list of voices in the second paragraph have on the reader?

   ....

   ....
   (1 mark)

4. How does the final paragraph make you feel? Explain your answer.

   ....

   ....
   (2 marks)

Spelling, Punctuation & Grammar Question

5. Write the plural of each underlined noun on the dotted lines.

   a) My friends are playing <u>elf</u> in this year's pantomime. ....

   b) My cousins auditioned to play the role of the <u>thief</u>. ....

   c) The actors will certainly have the time of their <u>life</u>. ....

   (3 marks)

Writing Question

6. Read the story prompt below.

   > A teenager is onstage at a talent show when a scream is heard from backstage.

   a) What mood could this story have? How would you create this mood?

   ....

   ....

   ....

   ....

   (2 marks)

   b) Think of a main character for the story. Describe two features of their personality.

   ....

   ....

   ....

   ....

   (2 marks)

Score: /12

Autumn Term: Workout 5

Warm up

1. Why should you use facts when you're writing to argue?

   ....

   (1 mark)

Reading Questions

> Dear General Manager of 'The Brill Grill',
>
> I am writing to pass on some concerns I had whilst dining at your restaurant last week.
>
> I am a regular customer of your restaurant and have previously found it to be of outstanding quality, so I was surprised to receive such a poor level of service this time around. Our food was extremely delayed (taking the best part of two hours to arrive), it wasn't heated through and I was presented with the wrong dish by your waiting staff.
>
> I expected a vastly different experience given your establishment's reputation, so I am confident you will take all the necessary measures to ensure this does not happen again.
>
> Yours faithfully,
>
> Mr Ewan Pritchard

2. a) Which of the following best describes the writer's tone? Circle one.

   | confused | bitter | threatening | critical |

   b) Explain your answer to part a).

   ....

   ....

   (2 marks)

3. Do you think the text's tone is appropriate for its purpose? Explain your answer.

   ....

   ....

   (1 mark)

Spelling, Punctuation & Grammar Question

4. Add a comma in the correct place in each sentence below.

   a) On Friday we have a reservation for dinner at the local pub.

   b) At the back of the café there is a grand piano that diners can play.

   c) Without warning the critic stood up and stormed out of the eatery.

   (3 marks)

Writing Questions

5. Imagine you are a food blogger. Write a short review of a local restaurant for your blog, telling your readers why they **should** or **shouldn't** eat there. Use alliteration, a rhetorical question and a list of three to persuade your readers.

   ....

   ....

   ....

   ....

   ....

   (3 marks)

6. Imagine a local café often over-buys food, only to throw lots of it away unused. Write the opening paragraph of a letter to the café, arguing for them to cut down on their food waste. Use emotive language and at least one fact in your writing.

   ....

   ....

   ....

   ....

   ....

   (2 marks)

Score: /12

Autumn Term: Workout 6

Warm up

1. Which of the following is **not** an adverb? Circle the correct option.

   sometimes   immediately   lonely   accidentally

   (1 mark)

Reading Questions

In sun-baked fields of petals bright,
He flits from flower to flower.
His papery wings grow wearier,
With each solitary hour.

He scans the rows of dahlias,
Origami heads all spent.
Not one drop left for me, he thinks,
While the others fly home content.

The glow of evening light descends,
And too, his deepest fears.
Then — a distant buzz of life,
And through the stalks, she appears.

She does a neat and sprightly dance,
And gone is his despair.
One store of treasured nectar,
Remains to satisfy the pair.

2. The dahlia flowers have "Origami heads". What does this suggest?

   ....

   ....
   (1 mark)

3. Why are the dahlias' heads described as "all spent"?

   ....
   (1 mark)

4. Reread the final stanza of the poem.
   Explain what happens in this stanza using your own words.

   ....

   ....
   (2 marks)

Spelling, Punctuation & Grammar Question

5. Underline the two adverbs in each sentence below.

    a) The beekeeper put the hive nearby so that he could talk to his bees often.

    b) The bee flew swiftly to the flower and landed softly on the yellow petal.

    c) The honey that I bought at the market is quite sweet and really fragrant.

    (3 marks)

Writing Questions

6. Read the lines below, which are from a different poem. Add two more lines to the poem, matching the rhythm used in the first pair of lines.

    > Billy Bean dreams of keeping bees,
    > A swarm to call his own.

    The rhythm of a line is how many syllables it has and the pattern of how those syllables are stressed.

    ....

    ....
    (2 marks)

7. Here are some more lines from the same poem. Rewrite them, using descriptive language to make them more interesting. Match the rhythm used in the pair of lines in question 6.

    > The sky turned a nice shade of blue,
    > And wind moved blades of grass.

    ....

    ....
    (2 marks)

Score: /12

Autumn Term: Workout 7

Warm up

1. Who is the protagonist of a text? Tick the correct option.

   the villain ☐   the narrator ☐   the main character ☐

   (1 mark)

Reading Questions

An isolated boarding school in the countryside, late at night. While the other boarders are asleep, **SABINA** *and* **FERGUS** *are looking for a book in the library.*

SABINA   *(running her finger along the book spines on a shelf)* Vampires, werewolves, zombies... Where is it? It must be here somewhere...

FERGUS   *(biting his lip and glancing around)* Wrong end of the alphabet, Sab.

SABINA   Oh. Hmm... Are ghouls the same thing? *(excitedly)* A-ha! I've got it!

SABINA *opens the book. As she does, a pale boy in an old-fashioned school uniform materialises by the bookshelf.* **SABINA** *and* **FERGUS** *spring back at the sight of him.*

BOY   *(grinning)* Pleasure to make your acquaintance. Don't let Mrs Robinson catch you in here at night!

2. a) How do you think Fergus feels about being in the library? Support your answer using evidence from the text.

   ....

   ....
   (2 marks)

   b) Explain why you think Fergus might feel this way.

   ....
   (1 mark)

3. What do you think the boy is? Explain your answer using evidence from the text.

   ....

   ....
   (2 marks)

Spelling, Punctuation & Grammar Question

4. Fill in the gap in each sentence using either 'our' or 'are'.

   a) We .... looking for books about witches.

   b) My neighbour claims that .... house is haunted.

   c) .... class is going ghost hunting next weekend.

   (3 marks)

Writing Question

5. The writer of the script on the previous page has made a plan for how the story continues. Use the plan to write the next part of the script, adding detail for each point. Use stage directions as well as dialogue.

   - *Fergus is scared and asks the boy what he's doing there.*
   - *Sabina is unnerved but tells Fergus not to be afraid.*
   - *The boy asks if he can have a tour of the school, as he hasn't looked around in a while.*

   ....

   ....

   ....

   ....

   ....

   ....

   ....

   ....

   (3 marks)

Score: /12

Autumn Term: Workout 8

Warm up

1. Tick the words below that are spelt correctly.

    confussion ☐   profession ☐   session ☐   decission ☐

    (1 mark)

Reading Questions

A At last we can announce that, after months of hold-ups, our bakery will be opening its doors once again THIS FRIDAY from 9 am. We look forward to seeing some familiar faces! Thanks everyone for your patience over the last year — we hope you're ready for your town to be back in the bread business!

B A passion for high-quality baking is at the heart of what we do, so we only use carefully sourced ingredients in our bread, which is handcrafted by our expert bakers each day. We now ship our renowned rustic bread nationwide, so you can experience the finest loaves that you've always wanted to try.

2. a) Which text is aimed at people who live near a specific bakery?

   ....

   b) Explain how you know this text is aimed at an audience local to the bakery.

   ....

   ....

   (2 marks)

3. a) What kind of audience would the other text be suitable for?

   ....

   b) Explain your answer to part a) using evidence from the text.

   ....

   ....

   (2 marks)

Spelling, Punctuation & Grammar Question

4. Complete each word using either 'cian', 'ssion' or 'tion'.

   Dubbed 'the pastry magi............ ', Monsieur Boulangerie has made quite the impre............ due to his objec............ to tradi............ . "I am a baking techni............ ! My mi............ is to find new flavours!" he insists.

   (3 marks)

Writing Question

5. The extract below is from an advert for a local bakery.

   > Are you craving a scrumptious sweet treat? Or are you hungry for a hearty homemade pie? Here at 'Smart Cookie', our family-run bakery, we pride ourselves on the love and care that goes into every baked good we produce.

   a) Write a short, snappy slogan that could go at the start of the advert.

   ....
   (1 mark)

   b) Write a final persuasive sentence for the advert that includes an opinion.

   ....
   ....
   (1 mark)

   c) Imagine the bakery has invented a new dessert. Write a short advert persuading people to buy this dessert. Use emotive language and a list of three.

   ....
   ....
   ....
   ....
   (2 marks)

   Score: / 12

Autumn Term: Workout 9

Warm up

1. What does the word 'summarise' mean?

   ....

   (1 mark)

Reading Questions

> Arlo crept warily through the forest, his trembling hands ripping leaves from drooping branches and tearing them into soft shards of green. As the trees began to thin out, he stopped and steadied his breathing, aware he was mere minutes from the enemy's base, where he was about to walk headfirst into danger.
>
> All he could think about was the look in his grandma's eyes when their food supply had run out, though whether her panic had been more at the thought of starvation or of him leaving to find food, he didn't know. They could only tolerate life hidden away in their cabin because they had each other, but now he had to risk it all — risk his life — to steal food from the enemy. She was his reason to keep going, his reminder that he couldn't give up no matter what. After getting so far, letting her down wasn't an option.

2. a) In your own words, summarise Arlo's feelings in the first paragraph.

   ....

   b) Find a quote that supports your answer to part a).

   ....

   (2 marks)

3. Explain why Arlo has left the cabin.

   ....

   ....

   (1 mark)

4. Write one sentence summarising the relationship between Arlo and his grandma.

   ....

   (1 mark)

Spelling, Punctuation & Grammar Question

5. The story continues below. Underline the three adjectives. Circle the three adverbs.

> Soon, he would have to be brave and walk fast with his hood up to avoid attracting unwanted attention. He had practised the plan countless times, hoping desperately to succeed.

(3 marks)

Writing Questions

6. The next four sentences of the story have been jumbled up.
   Write the numbers 1-4 in the boxes to put them in the correct order.

   He crouched down behind a bush, hearing a raspy voice begin to speak. ☐

   "They'll find it mightily difficult to hide from me," another voice replied. ☐

   "Keep an eye out for fugitives — there's always some lurking in the forest." ☐

   Arlo was brought out of his thoughts by the sound of rustling in the trees. ☐

   (1 mark)

7. Use bullet points to plan out the next four plot points of the story.
   Structure the story so the atmosphere becomes more tense.

   ....

   ....

   ....

   ....

   ....

   ....

   ....

   (3 marks)

Score: ☐ / 12

Autumn Term: Workout 10

Warm up

1. What is the most likely purpose of a text that uses hyperbole?

   to inform   to advise   to explain   to persuade

   (1 mark)

Reading Question

A Many households in the UK were slow to adopt colour television. Although the UK's first broadcast in colour (that of the Wimbledon tennis tournament) was in 1967, colour TV sets only became more popular than black and white sets in 1976.

B <u>Troubleshooting</u>
If you find that your device is struggling to connect to the Internet, try turning it off and on again. You'll often find that a simple reboot of your equipment can solve many different internet connection issues.

C We can't ignore the consistent evidence that shows excessive use of smartphones is damaging to our mental health. Stress, anxiety, poor sleep... Must I go on? We need to wake up and recognise the risks.

2. a) Match each text to its purpose by writing A, B or C in the boxes below.

   to advise ☐   to argue ☐   to inform ☐

   (1 mark)

   b) Name a feature of Text A and Text B that supports your answer to part a).

   Text A ....

   Text B ....

   (1 mark)

   c) Choose one feature from Text C and explain why it suits the text's purpose.

   ....

   ....

   (2 marks)

Spelling, Punctuation & Grammar Question

3. Add a colon in the correct place in each sentence below.

   a) There is one huge reason why I'm afraid of robots sci-fi films.

   b) I need two things a computer keyboard and a monitor.

   c) I slammed the laptop shut I had finally finished my homework.

   (3 marks)

Writing Question

4. a) Choose one of the prompts below, then write two points arguing in favour of it.

   | Limiting time spent on social media | Enforcing an age limit on owning a phone | Using tablets in the classroom |

   - ....

   - ....
   (1 mark)

   b) Now write two points arguing against the prompt.

   - ....

   - ....
   (1 mark)

   c) Choose one of your points from above, then write an essay paragraph based on that point. Make sure your paragraph has a clear structure and that you add detail to support your point.

   ....

   ....

   ....

   ....
   (2 marks)

   Score: ☐ /12

Autumn Term: Workout 11

Warm up

1. Name one thing that a preposition can tell you.

   ....

   (1 mark)

Reading Questions

> She's been away for many years,
> A self-imposed exile,
> Chasing goals and hopes and dreams,
> That don't grow on that tiny isle.
>
> The soil could not sustain their life,
> She felt them struggling for air,
> Ambitions losing consciousness,
> A frightening, rare health scare.
>
> The doctor took one look at her,
> And prescribed a quick escape.
> She left the isle for city lights,
> Where her dreams at last took shape.
>
> But now and then, she questions if
> The dose was much too strong.
> Was the treatment too extreme?
> Did the doctor get it wrong?

2. a) In your own words, explain why the woman wanted to leave the island.

   ....

   ....

   b) Write down a quote from the poem that supports your answer to part a).

   ....

   ....

   (2 marks)

3. What happens in the final stanza? Tick a box.

   The woman considers whether she should see a new doctor. ☐

   The woman contemplates whether she should move to a new city. ☐

   The woman wonders whether she should have left the island. ☐

   (1 mark)

Spelling, Punctuation & Grammar Question

4. Underline the eight prepositions in the extract below.

> Living *on* an island is phenomenal. People who don't live *near* the sea rarely see the ocean, but I live *beside* it, so the sight is a familiar one. Every day, I head *to* the beach *with* my dog and witness the sun emerging *over* the horizon. The sand sinks *between* my toes as the waves lap *at* the shore.

(4 marks)

Writing Question

5. Read the first two lines of the poem below.

> The fresh island air,
> That grazes my skin.

Using the same rhythm as these lines, write your own lines to come after each of the lines below.

The sand on my toes,

....

The crash of the waves,

....

The scent of the palms,

....

The warmth of the sun,

....

(4 marks)

Score: /12

Autumn Term: Workout 12

Warm up

1. Give three words that are examples of onomatopoeia.

   ....

   (1 mark)

Reading Questions

> As she grasped her harness, Zuri's heart was a pounding drum. Amidst the deafening silence of the cockpit, it was the only thing she could hear. Despite knowing the engineers were experts, they had strapped her in a little too quickly. A more thorough inspection would have been appreciated, given the extremely high stakes.
>
> "Five seconds to launch," she heard as she squeezed her eyes shut.
>
> The spaceship coughed and spluttered, then whipped into the air and whistled and whooshed and whizzed and whirred around like it was painting a frenzied picture out of steam on the canvas of the night sky.

2. Circle the technique found in the phrase "the deafening silence of the cockpit".

   | personification | repetition | oxymoron | simile |

   (1 mark)

3. Write down a metaphor from the text above and explain its effect.

   ....

   ....

   (1 mark)

4. a) The final sentence doesn't use much punctuation. What is the effect of this?

   ....

   b) Name two more language techniques that are used in the final sentence.

   ....

   (2 marks)

Autumn Term: Workout 12

Spelling, Punctuation & Grammar Question

5. Write whether the underlined part of the sentence is a clause or a phrase.

    a) I watched <u>the comet in the distance</u> come closer. ....

    b) <u>As we took off</u>, I said a silent prayer to myself. ....

    c) I gazed down longingly at <u>our planet below</u>. ....

    (3 marks)

Writing Questions

6. Rewrite the sentences below so that each one uses a simile to create the same meaning.

    a) **The stars twinkled brightly.**

    ....

    b) **The alien looked frightened.**

    ....

    (2 marks)

7. Imagine you have just landed on the Moon.

    a) Write a sentence that uses a metaphor to describe what you see.

    ....

    ....

    b) Write a sentence that uses hyperbole (exaggeration) to describe how you feel.

    ....

    ....

    (2 marks)

Score: /12

Spring Term: Workout 1

Warm up

1. Give one layout feature that you would expect to see in a newspaper article.

   ....

   (1 mark)

Reading Questions

THE NUMBER ONE BESTSELLER IN SELF-HELP

Ready for a change of tune? Keen to march to the beat of your own drum?

Drawing on her years of experience as a music psychologist, Dr Song shares all the tips and tricks you need to fine-tune your life.

★★★★★
"The BEST self-help book on the market"
The Help Journal

★★★★
"A phenomenally practical and useful book"
CONFIDENCE Magazine

2. The text's first line is in a box. Why do you think the writer made this line stand out?

   ....

   (1 mark)

3. Look at the two paragraphs above the star ratings. Why do you think the writer has ordered the ideas in these paragraphs in this way?

   ....

   ....

   (1 mark)

4. Explain why you think the writer put *The Help Journal*'s review first. Use evidence from the text in your answer.

   ....

   ....

   (2 marks)

Spelling, Punctuation & Grammar Question

5. Circle the correct word to complete each sentence below.

   a) The new album **by** / **bye** / **buy** Melody Funk is the best album of the year.

   b) I'm saving up to **by** / **bye** / **buy** tickets to see my favourite singer live.

   c) Rex left to go on tour with his band and he didn't even say **by** / **bye** / **buy** .

   (3 marks)

Writing Questions

6. The extract on the left is from a newspaper article.
   The extract on the right is from an essay about the article.

Lee's third album continues in that same fairylike spirit, threading angelic harmonies into the verses.	The article says the album "has a fairylike spirit". This, along with its angelic harmonies, creates a whimsical feel.

   Rewrite the essay extract so that the quotes are punctuated correctly.

   ....

   ....
   (2 marks)

7. Answer the questions, embedding a quote from the extract below in each answer.

   > Pop-up dance floors have been springing up in city centres all over the country this week as part of a new government scheme to get the nation dancing.

   a) Where are the dance floors appearing?

   ....

   b) Why has the government introduced pop-up dance floors?

   ....
   (2 marks)

Score: ☐ / 12

Spring Term: Workout 2

> **Warm up**
>
> 1. Name three possible traits of a character who works as a dog walker.
>
>   ....
>
>   *(1 mark)*

Reading Questions

> Miss Fenwick's neighbours described her as a social butterfly. Dressed head to toe in mismatched patterns, she would squeal "Yoohoo!" at any unsuspecting person she bumped into whilst out walking her bubblegum-tinted poodle. Her hair was curled into ringlets that framed a toothy smile, which resided on her face day and night.
>
> Every day, Miss Fenwick passed Mr Halpert clipping his hedges. He would roll his eyes at her zest for life, muttering that it would surely run out soon enough.
>
> "Yoohoo!" she would call extra loudly at the sight of him, smiling softly to herself as he toiled away in his garden. "Care for a helping hand, Mr Halpert?"

2. a) Explain what the description "social butterfly" means.

   ....

   b) Write down one thing about Miss Fenwick that shows she is a "social butterfly".

   ....

   (2 marks)

3. Mr Halpert "would roll his eyes" at Miss Fenwick's "zest for life".
   What does this suggest about Mr Halpert's character?

   ....

   (1 mark)

4. How do you think Miss Fenwick feels about Mr Halpert? Explain your answer.

   ....

   ....

   (2 marks)

Spelling, Punctuation & Grammar Question

5. Add a pair of commas to each sentence to show which bit is extra information.

   a) That cottage the home of Mr Halpert is over 300 years old.

   b) Miss Fenwick beaming from ear to ear commended its beauty.

   c) Her impatient poodle quick to get bored tugged on its lead.

   (3 marks)

Writing Question

6. Here is the next part of the story.

   > One day, Mr Chen, a new resident, found a box of cookies on his doorstep, welcoming him to the area. As he bent down to pick them up, Miss Fenwick's poodle bounded over the fence and inhaled the cookies in one quick bite.

   Write the next sentence of the story to show how Mr Chen would react if he was:

   Think about how you could use Mr Chen's actions and appearance to get across his character.

   a) good-natured

   ....

   ....

   b) quick to anger

   ....

   ....

   c) anxious

   ....

   ....

   (3 marks)

   Score: ☐ / 12

Spring Term: Workout 3

Warm up

1. What does it mean to scan a text?

   ....
   (1 mark)

Reading Questions

> There is no better reason than a boat trip to pull yourself away from whichever charming resort you have chosen to stay at in Kefalonia. We found it to be the perfect way of exploring this Greek island's natural beauty.
>
> Gliding on the crystal blue ocean, we passed quaint, sleepy villages; white, sandy beaches; and mystifying, hidden caves, all just a stone's throw from our hotel. We set sail on a particularly sticky day, so I was tempted to take a dip in the caves' pools. However, our tour guide was on a tight schedule to show us all the sights, so we couldn't stay anywhere for long. Despite this, my overall experience was positive — few other places have enthralled me as much as the idyllic Kefalonian landscape that we were blessed to see on this day!

2. a) Which word best summarises how the writer feels about Kefalonia as a place?

   | surprised | captivated | overwhelmed | inspired |

   b) Explain your answer to part a) using evidence from the text.

   ....

   ....
   (2 marks)

3. Summarise the positive and negative parts of the writer's day out in Kefalonia.

   ....

   ....

   ....
   (2 marks)

Spelling, Punctuation & Grammar Question

4. Fill in the gaps in each sentence using either 'don't' or 'doesn't'.

   a) Ella's grandad .... speak Greek at home, so she .... know any.

   b) Why .... we go to Corfu instead? The journey .... take as long.

   (2 marks)

Writing Questions

5. Redraft this text so it uses more interesting vocabulary and sentence structures.

   > The best thing about Greece is the food because it is really delicious and there are lots of nice restaurants where you can try a variety of traditional Greek dishes.

   ....

   ....

   ....

   ....

   (2 marks)

6. Proofread this extract from a travel blog about Greece.
   Circle the six mistakes and write the correction above each one.

   > I have found athens in particular to be a simply breathtaking city, brimming with
   >
   > fasinating museums, magnificent building's and rich culture. The Parthenon is
   >
   > just as you see it in pictures; it was a absolute treat to visit this anceint structure.
   >
   > I could of looked at it for ages, but I had to meet up with my friend for dinner.

   (3 marks)

   Score: /12

Spring Term: Workout 4

Warm up

1. What is free verse?

   ....

   (1 mark)

Reading Questions

> Time summons a wrinkle or two;
> They spread like cracks on ice.
> The first fall of snow comes when
> Locks of my hair glisten silver,
> Though I fear I'm worth less than that.
>
> Before long, it's all fallen out;
> The tree has lost its leaves.
> My skin starts to droop and
> I'm reminded I'm no longer a lamb.
> It's bitterly cold, getting old.

2. "Locks of my hair glisten silver, / Though I fear I'm worth less than that."
   What do these lines tell you about the narrator's thoughts on ageing?

   ....

   ....

   (1 mark)

3. How does the poet use language to make ageing seem like a sad process?

   ....

   ....

   (1 mark)

4. Why do you think the poet uses imagery related to winter? Explain your answer.

   ....

   ....

   ....

   (2 marks)

Spelling, Punctuation & Grammar Question

5. Tick or cross each sentence to show whether it uses an apostrophe correctly.

    a) The two chicks' beaks were open wide. ☐

    b) A colony of honey bees' buzzed around the flowers. ☐

    c) Those tree's leaves have turned golden brown. ☐

    d) The three women's gardens were covered in snow. ☐

    (4 marks)

Writing Question

6. Here is a rhyming couplet about summer. Write three more rhyming couplets about autumn, winter and spring to make a complete poem about the seasons.

    > *Blazing sun and blooming flowers,*
    > *Sitting out until the evening hours.*

    Autumn: ....

    ....

    Winter: ....

    ....

    Spring: ....

    ....

    (3 marks)

Score: ☐ /12

Spring Term: Workout 5

> **Warm up**
>
> 1. Give one adjective to describe the mood of the sentence below.
>
>   **I gazed out at the city sleeping blissfully in perfect tranquillity.** ....
>
>   *(1 mark)*

Reading Questions

> The impatient honk of horns echoed up and down the street. All around Annie, city dwellers hurried through the rain, urgency coursing through their veins, shoes clacking against the pavement like the dull but persistent ticking of a clock. Annie cast them a glance, hoping for a smile that never came. Instead, she was met with an expression alien to her — the vacant stare of people ruled by tight schedules.
>
> She gazed up at the skyscrapers that reigned over the city. They looked straight over her, refusing to acknowledge an outsider. She turned to the traffic lights for approval, but upon seeing her, they rolled their eyes to red in unmistakable hostility.

2. Write down a quote from the text that suggests Annie is in an unfamiliar place.

   ....
   (1 mark)

3. a) Circle the word that best summarises the setting of the extract above.

   | neglected | chilling | unwelcoming | treacherous |

   b) Explain your answer to part a) using evidence from the text.

   ....

   ....
   (2 marks)

4. How is the city presented as a place where people are pressed for time?

   ....

   ....
   (1 mark)

Spelling, Punctuation & Grammar Question

5. Underline the two words in each sentence that should be joined by a hyphen. Then rewrite the hyphenated word on the dotted line.

   a) It took all my self control not to scream at the traffic. ....

   b) The city's ex mayor resigned from her role last year. ....

   c) There are long term plans to create more cycle lanes. ....
   (3 marks)

Writing Questions

6. Rewrite the following description so it's appropriate for a story set in an abandoned city. Use language that creates an eerie atmosphere.

   > Lofty buildings and bustling crowds seemed to close in on me. Turning down a side street, I passed sparkling café windows, hearing friendly conversation from within.

   ....

   ....

   ....
   (2 marks)

7. Choose a story title from below. Write the first paragraph of the story, in which you create a specific atmosphere through your description of the setting.

   | Wilderness Wonders | Going for Gold | Haunted Hideaway |

   ....

   ....

   ....

   ....

   ....
   (2 marks)

Score: /12

Spring Term: Workout 6

Warm up

1. Give two language features that you might use when writing to advise.

   ....

   (1 mark)

Reading Questions

> Thinking back to my first day training on the wards, all I remember is feeling pure adrenaline. Nothing could have prepared me for it — the hours I'd spent studying healthcare manuals and textbooks certainly hadn't.
>
> The truth is, they throw you in head-first at the deep end. It's up to you whether you sink or swim. That first day, I was nearly drowning, desperately trying to keep my head above the surface — not just for me, but for my patients too. Then, bit by bit, it took a little less effort to tread water, and eventually I learnt how to float. Helping the doctors to care for those in need was an experience like no other. Though a life on the wards is a tough grind, and the quiet moments waiting for something to happen can be even worse, there aren't many jobs that are more gratifying than this one.

2. What job is being described in the text above? How can you tell?

   ....

   ....
   (1 mark)

3. The writer had been "studying" books for "hours" before starting their job. What does this suggest about their personality?

   ....
   (1 mark)

4. How did the writer initially manage their job? Explain your answer.

   ....

   ....
   (2 marks)

Spelling, Punctuation & Grammar Question

5. Write 'F' or 'I' to show whether each sentence uses formal or informal language.

   a) Regrettably, the deadline for this job posting has now passed.   ....

   b) My colleague owes me one for covering his shift last week.   ....

   c) Being in part-time employment gives me the best of both worlds.   ....

   (3 marks)

Writing Questions

6. a) Imagine you are a paramedic who works in the ambulance service. You are going into a secondary school to give a talk informing pupils about your job. Write a short introduction to your speech that includes one fact about your role.

   ....

   ....

   ....

   (1 mark)

   b) Now explain one trait that would make someone a good fit for this role.

   ....

   ....

   (1 mark)

7. Finish your speech by giving advice to anyone interested in a career as a paramedic. Use second-person pronouns and a reassuring tone.

   ....

   ....

   ....

   ....

   (2 marks)

   Score: ☐ /12

Spring Term: Workout 7

Warm up

1. What is a simile?

   ....

   (1 mark)

Reading Questions

> Dark spruce forest frowned on either side the frozen waterway. The trees had been stripped by a recent wind of their white covering of frost, and they seemed to lean towards each other, black and ominous, in the fading light. A vast silence reigned over the land. The land itself was a desolation, lifeless, without movement, so lone and cold that the spirit of it was not even that of sadness. There was a hint in it of laughter, but of a laughter more terrible than any sadness—a laughter that was mirthless* as the smile of the sphinx, a laughter cold as the frost and partaking of the grimness of infallibility**.

*mirthless — *joyless*   **infallibility — *always being right*

An extract from *White Fang* by Jack London

2. Write down an example of a simile from the text above.

   ....

   (1 mark)

3. a) Circle the technique used in the phrase "Dark spruce forest frowned".

   | oxymoron | irony | onomatopoeia | personification |

   b) What impression of the forest does this create?

   ....

   (2 marks)

4. How does the text's use of adjectives make the setting seem dangerous? Refer to two adjectives in your answer.

   ....

   ....

   (2 marks)

Spelling, Punctuation & Grammar Question

Use a coordinating conjunction to join each pair of sentences together.

5. Rewrite each pair of sentences as a compound sentence.

   a) The river was cold. The wolf swam across anyway.

   ....

   b) I don't want to go outside. There is a snowstorm.

   ....
   (2 marks)

Writing Questions

6. Proofread this extract from a different story set in the wilderness. Circle the six mistakes and write the correction above each one.

   > The snow persisted all night; never lessening or pausing. Little by little, the track was coverred over. When we waked up, Alia and me saw that the track had become to indistinct to follow, so we wouldnt be able to reach the town.

   (2 marks)

7. Redraft this text so it uses more interesting vocabulary and sentence structures.

   > The man woke up. He looked around him. He began to panic.
   > The world was white with snow. He had no idea which way to go.

   ....
   ....
   ....
   ....
   ....
   (2 marks)

Score: /12

Spring Term: Workout 8

Warm up

1. What is a counter-argument?

   ....
   (1 mark)

Reading Questions

ARJUN DAZZLES IN NEW THRILLER

Arjun has brought yet another eye-popping, blood-rushing and head-spinning performance to the big screen this week with his self-directed film, *Code Name*.

In this awfully good thriller, Arjun takes on the role of a spy posing as a cleaner at a government headquarters who uncovers state secrets and international conspiracies.

Arjun's suspenseful escapades make the film nothing less than gripping, and with cameos from his Hollywood friends, this motion picture has well and truly cracked the code. It's certainly no secret that a host of awards will be knocking at Arjun's door this year.

And another thing's for sure — Arjun has taken to the director's chair like a duck to water. But it does beg the question: will Arjun *ever* put a foot wrong?

2. Which language technique is used in each of these examples from the text?

   In this awfully good thriller → ....

   awards will be knocking at Arjun's door → ....
   (2 marks)

3. Explain the effect created by the rhetorical question at the end of the text.

   ....

   ....
   (1 mark)

4. Write down an example of a list of three from the text. Explain its effect.

   ....

   ....
   (2 marks)

Spelling, Punctuation & Grammar Question

5. Add a pair of brackets to each sentence to show which bit is extra information.

   a) The cinema is handing out free buckets of popcorn the sweet variety to encourage passersby to come in and buy a ticket .

   b) Flick Clément who is a famous actor is best known for her portrayal of a young mathematician in *The Power of 10* .

   (2 marks)

Writing Question

6. Imagine you are planning to write an essay with the following title:
   'Drama should be a bigger part of the school curriculum. How far do you agree?'

   a) Write down two points you could make to support the statement.

   • ....
   • ....
   (1 mark)

   b) Write down two points you could make to challenge the statement.

   • ....
   • ....
   (1 mark)

   c) Choose one of your points from above, then write an essay paragraph based on that point. Make sure your paragraph has a clear structure and that you add detail to support your point.

   ....
   ....
   ....
   ....
   ....
   (2 marks)

   Score: /12

Spring Term: Workout 9

Warm up

1. Underline the three adjectives in the following sentence.

   The mighty waterfall tumbled loudly from the steep cliff; it was quite stunning.

   (1 mark)

Reading Questions

People come and people go,	Gases rise from fiery deep,
But here I stand, unchanging.	But still I stand, unchanging.
Warm days pass, and days of snow,	From within, they start to creep,
But here I stand, unchanging.	But still I stand, unchanging.
From my peak, they praise the view,	Then a crack like thunder rends the sky,
And still I stand, unchanging.	Rivers of fire from me fly,
I've seen the old and the new,	Dormant I no longer lie!
And still I stand, unchanging.	And you thought me unchanging?

2. Who or what is the narrator of the poem above?

   ....

   (1 mark)

3. In the poem's final line, the narrator addresses the reader. What is the effect of this?

   ....

   (1 mark)

4. The poem includes the lines "But here I stand, unchanging" and "Dormant I no longer lie!" What tone is created by each of these lines?

   ....

   ....

   ....

   (2 marks)

Spelling, Punctuation & Grammar Question

5. Add a colon or a semicolon in the correct place in each sentence below.

   a) We need three things in our survival kit water, food and medicine.

   b) Jonny climbed all the way to the top Ravinder stayed at the bottom.

   (2 marks)

Writing Questions

6. The following poem is about a desert. Replace each adjective in brackets with a more interesting adjective that has a similar meaning.

   The (**hot**) .... sun beats down

   Upon the (**dry**) .... earth below.

   A (**big**) .... space, lifeless and void,

   The wind's (**sad**) .... sigh the only sound.

   (2 marks)

7. Write your own four-line poem about a cave. In your poem, you should use:

   | the future tense | interesting adjectives | first-person narration |

   ....

   ....

   ....

   ....

   (3 marks)

Score: ☐ / 12

Spring Term: Workout 10

Warm up

1. Why might a writer use a flashback in a piece of fiction?

   ....

   (1 mark)

Reading Questions

> I interviewed the cook first: *"Why, Detective. I was in the drawing room when the clock struck midnight. There was a piercing scream on the landing upstairs, and then a loud thud."*
>
> Next came Master Jeffries: *"I rushed up the staircase shortly after midnight and that's when I saw the body. Terrible shame, isn't it? She was a dear friend to me. Well, will that be all?"*
>
> Then I spoke to Davis, the butler: *"I hurried out of the kitchen and along the secret passage, then I heard the clock chime twelve times. I entered the drawing room to find Lord Sutcliffe alone, smoking a pipe. I'd say that serves as a credible alibi for us both, don't you think?"*
>
> Lord Sutcliffe was last to be interviewed: *"That's right, Davis joined me just after midnight. We both heard the scream. Mind if I pour myself a drink, old chap? It's been quite a night..."*
>
> So you see, their stories just didn't add up...

2. Master Jeffries says, "Well, will that be all?" immediately after saying, "She was a dear friend to me." What does this suggest?

   ....

   (1 mark)

3. The writer reveals information about the murder bit by bit. What is the effect of this?

   ....

   ....

   (1 mark)

4. What effect does the narrator's final line have on the reader? Explain your answer.

   ....

   ....

   (2 marks)

Spelling, Punctuation & Grammar Question

5. Underline each incorrectly spelt word in the extract below, then write the correct spelling above it.

> Sutcliffe Manor's cook, Cassie Role, keeps the ressipe for her famous 'Death by Chocolate' cake consealed. I resently had a slice — it truly is a killer dessert!

(3 marks)

Writing Question

6. Read Mrs Role's diary entry from the night before the murder. Rewrite it, correcting any spelling, punctuation or grammar mistakes and adding your own descriptive words where the ink has smudged.

> I have decided that tomorrow shall be the day. I have dealed with her ▓▓▓▓ demands for far too long. She has rejects every dish I serve. "It could use a pinch of salt, she announces smuggly. Well, I refuse to except this impolite behaviour. I will strike when everyone is drowsy from all the food and the port. Yes, its going to be ▓▓▓▓.

....
....
....
....
....
....
....

(4 marks)

Score: /12

Spring Term: Workout 11

Warm up

1. Why should you use emotive language when you are writing to persuade?

   ....

   (1 mark)

Reading Questions

A **ALLEN & GRIFFITHS**

Bringing you all of the latest fashions, Allen & Griffiths are the ladies' tailor of choice. We have assembled the most splendid collection of gowns in the known universe, made from only the finest, hand-sewn silks and inspired by designs popular in Paris. If you wish to be the most stylish guest at any party, you simply must visit Allen & Griffiths.

B Dear Owner of 'Breathtaking Brides',

I am writing to tell you how thoroughly disheartened I am with the dress I purchased from your shop. The garment's poor quality quite frankly sabotaged my entire wedding! A thread came loose on the dance floor, causing the biggest catastrophe of my entire life. I therefore await the payment of a full refund.

Yours faithfully, Mrs Slatcher

2. Circle the technique used by both texts to persuade the reader.

   simile   onomatopoeia   pun   hyperbole (exaggeration)

   (1 mark)

3. Compare the tone of Text A to the tone of Text B.

   ....

   ....

   (1 mark)

4. Both texts use second-person narration to address the reader. What effect does this have in Text A compared to in Text B?

   ....

   ....

   ....

   (2 marks)

Spelling, Punctuation & Grammar Question

5. Add dashes in the correct places in each sentence below.

    a) Jim my friend from school knitted me a scarf for my birthday.

    b) The two shopkeepers Layla and Kioshi always get to work early.

    c) Midori lost her favourite piece of jewellery her necklace yesterday.

    (3 marks)

Writing Questions

6. Rewrite the advert below so it uses persuasive language to convince people to visit the shop.

    > We sell some jewellery as well as some watches. The prices of our items are okay, and you might find something you want to buy here.

    ....

    ....

    ....

    ....

    (2 marks)

7. The paragraph below argues against shopping online. Write a paragraph arguing in favour of shopping online, using techniques appropriate for writing to argue.

    > If you shop online, you can't try the clothes on before you buy them, so you don't know if they're going to be the right size for you. This means that you often have to return your items, which can be an inconvenience.

    ....

    ....

    ....

    ....

    (2 marks)

    Score: ☐ / 12

Spring Term: Workout 12

Warm up

1. Fill in the gaps in the sentence below, which is about the structure of plays.

   Plays are often divided into .... , which are divided into ....
   (1 mark)

Reading Questions

> *In the shadowy corridor of a museum,* **ARNIE** *shines his torch up and down.*
>
> **ARNIE**   Hello? Bob? *(sighs)* He's vanished. I'd be lying if I said this comes as a surprise.
>
> **ARNIE** *slinks stealthily around a corner and catches sight of* **BOB**, *who is transfixed by a dinosaur skeleton.* **ARNIE** *strides over to him and shines his torch directly in* **BOB**'s *eyes.*
>
> **BOB**   *(blinking furiously)* Ouch! Whaddya do that for?
>
> **ARNIE**   Put your eyes to good use, Bob! Time is of the essence! If we don't snag the necklace soon, we'll be leaving here in handcuffs. Now, did you pack my pair of white gloves?
>
> **BOB**   *(after a long pause)* Did you say *gloves*? With a 'g'?
>
> **BOB** *opens his rucksack slowly, releasing two white doves into the air.* **ARNIE** *groans. A deafening alarm begins to ring.* **ARNIE**'s *torch clatters to the floor.* **BOB** *winces.*

2. Why do you think Bob "*winces*" at the end of the extract?

   ....
   (1 mark)

3. What do you think Arnie thinks of Bob? Use evidence from the text in your answer.

   ....

   ....
   (2 marks)

4. How does the writer create humour through Bob and Arnie's characters?
   Use evidence from the text to explain your answer.

   ....

   ....
   (2 marks)

Spelling, Punctuation & Grammar Question

5. Here are some lines from later in the play. Fill in each gap with the correct form of the verb in brackets so the verb matches the tense of the text.

> **ARNIE** You .... *(have)* one job and you still .... *(mess)* it up.
>
> **BOB** Oh, stop .... *(worry)*. We won't get .... *(catch)*.
>
> **ARNIE** I .... *(tell)* you to keep your voice down. Now open that door.
>
> **BOB** Oops. I think I .... *(leave)* my crowbar in the van.

(3 marks)

Writing Question

6. The extract on the left is from a story. The extract on the right is from an essay about the story. Rewrite the essay extract so that the quotes are punctuated correctly.

> *Unfamiliar footsteps signal that the intruder is drawing closer. The floorboards make a startling creaking sound as they approach, and I dart behind the sofa as goosebumps prickle along my arms.*

> The intruder is presented as menacing. There is a "startling" creaking sound as they walk, which creates a tense atmosphere. The narrator, however, is portrayed as nervous. They "quickly dart" away to hide and "goosebumps prickle along my arms", which suggests they are panicked.

....

....

....

....

....

....

(3 marks)

Score: / 12

Summer Term: Workout 1

Warm up

1. Write 'F' or 'I' to show whether each text would use formal or informal language.

   a job application □   **a message to a friend** □   **a history essay** □   **a postcard** □

   (1 mark)

Reading Questions

> With their crispy exteriors and soft, fluffy insides, it is abundantly clear that roast potatoes are superior to all other forms of potato. Roast potatoes are, of course, the perfect addition to any roast dinner. And that's not all — their scrumptious flavour and nutritious nature makes them ideal for a mid-morning snack. Or perhaps you've woken up at 3 am, desperate to satisfy a gnawing in your stomach? If so, a good roastie is what you need.

2. Why do you think the writer of the text above used second-person pronouns?

   ....

   ....
   (1 mark)

3. How does the writer use sensory language? What effect does this have on your feelings about roast potatoes? Use evidence from the text in your answer.

   ....

   ....
   (2 marks)

4. The text is part of an advert written by Mary Piper, founder of Piper's Potatoes Ltd. How does knowing this affect your opinion of the text? Explain your answer.

   ....

   ....
   (2 marks)

Spelling, Punctuation & Grammar Question

5. Add the suffix to the root word. Write the correct spelling on the line.

   happy + ness = ...   copy + ing = ...

   wheezy + ly = ...   envy + ous = ...

   (2 marks)

Writing Question

6. The letter below is from Mr Edward King to Mary Piper of Piper's Potatoes Ltd. Rewrite it using informal language, addressing it from Edward to a friend instead.

   > Dear Ms Piper,
   > I am writing to inform you of my complete agreement with your article concerning the many merits of roast potatoes. It is my firm opinion that these foodstuffs complement almost any dish excellently. Indeed, when I dine at a restaurant, I object in the strongest possible terms if I find that the roast potatoes fall short of my lofty expectations — such is my strength of feeling regarding this humble food.
   > Yours sincerely,
   > Mr Edward King

   ....

   ....

   ....

   ....

   ....

   ....

   ....

   ....

   (4 marks)

Score: /12

Summer Term: Workout 2

Warm up

1. True or false? Metaphors compare something to something else using 'like' or 'as'.

   ....
   (1 mark)

Reading Questions

> These murky marshes have no master;
> Nature — we cannot outlast her.
> From all around, I feel her glare,
> Warning me to retreat faster.
>
> The trees' long arms, they yank my hair,
> The reeds cling to me everywhere.
> I row home quickly, out of fright,
> As water bellows, "Do you dare?"
>
> I hide from Nature, out of sight;
> Humans never win this fight.
> It's an age-old feud, I think,
> And we don't have the strongest bite.
>
> Nature grows and mortals shrink,
> Waters rise and rowboats sink.
> Nature — we cannot outlast her;
> She will not flinch, she will not blink.

2. a) The writer uses personification in the line "The trees' long arms, they yank my hair". What does this suggest about nature?

   ....

   ....
   (1 mark)

   b) Copy another example of personification from the poem and explain its effect.

   ....

   ....
   (2 marks)

3. What is the effect of repeating the line "Nature — we cannot outlast her"?

   ....

   ....
   (1 mark)

Spelling, Punctuation & Grammar Question

4. Circle the correct word to complete each sentence below.

   a) **Who's / Whose** going out on the boat today?

   b) I'm not sure **who's / whose** oar this is.

   c) I need to know **who's / whose** rowed before.

(3 marks)

Writing Questions

5. Each line of the poem below uses a colour to describe a feature of the landscape. Add two more lines to the poem, using two more colours to describe the scene. Use at least one language technique (e.g. personification, a simile) in each line.

   > Blue is the river, a ribbon of water,
   > Grey are the rocks, sitting resilient,

   ....

   ....

   (2 marks)

6. Choose something else you'd find in nature (e.g. a cloud or a tree), then write a four-line poem about it. Your poem should include at least two language techniques.

   ....

   ....

   ....

   ....

   (2 marks)

Score: ☐ / 12

Summer Term: Workout 3

Warm up

1. Give one reason why knowing the context of a fiction text is important.

   ....

   (1 mark)

Reading Questions

> "Ay, there she comes," continued Mrs. Bennet, "looking as unconcerned as may be, and caring no more for us than if we were at York, provided she can have her own way. But I tell you what, Miss Lizzy, if you take it into your head to go on refusing every offer of marriage in this way, you will never get a husband at all — and I am sure I do not know who is to maintain you when your father is dead. *I* shall not be able to keep you — and so I warn you. I have done with you from this very day. I told you in the library, you know, that I should never speak to you again, and you will find me as good as my word. I have no pleasure in talking to undutiful children."

An extract from *Pride and Prejudice* by Jane Austen

2. Copy a quote from the text that suggests Mrs. Bennet wants her daughter to obey her.

   ....

   (1 mark)

3. Mrs. Bennet tells Lizzy "*I* shall not be able to keep you — and so I warn you." What does this suggest about Mrs. Bennet's financial situation?

   ....

   ....

   (1 mark)

4. The extract above comes from a novel published in 1813. What does it suggest about marriage at the time? Use evidence from the extract in your answer.

   ....

   ....

   ....

   (2 marks)

Spelling, Punctuation & Grammar Question

5. Complete each word using either 'cious' or 'tious'.

    a) Mrs. Bennet is ambi............. and wants her daughter to marry a rich man.

    b) Lizzy is cau............. not to get married for the wrong reasons.

    c) Early editions of Jane Austen's novels are now very pre............. .

    (3 marks)

Writing Question

6. Write the opening paragraph of a story set 200 years ago. Think of a main character and an old-fashioned setting, then use descriptive language to describe both.
    For ideas about what life was like 200 years ago, have a look at the boxes below.

    > There was no electricity.

    > All healthcare cost money.

    > People travelled in horse-drawn carriages.

    ....

    ....

    ....

    ....

    ....

    ....

    ....

    ....

    ....

    (4 marks)

Score: ☐ / 12

Summer Term: Workout 4

Warm up

1. What is meant by the 'form' of a text? Circle one.

   | the order of its information | what type of text it is | what tone it uses |

   (1 mark)

Reading Questions

Have you only got limited time to explore Borton Castle? Here are our top three recommendations:

- **Watch** the knights do battle in our live **jousting shows** in the **lower courtyard**.
- **Climb** the 212 steps to the top of the **Great Tower** and enjoy **stunning views** of the Wembrian countryside.
- **Discover** the 12th-century **dungeon** where Lord William Hamersley was imprisoned for more than twenty years.

Under 5s go free!

2. Why do you think the writer chose to use bullet points in the text above?

   ....

   (1 mark)

3. The text includes a box that says "Under 5s go free!" Write down one thing about the layout of this box that makes it ineffective. Explain your answer.

   ....

   ....

   (2 marks)

4. Do you think the image of the castle is a useful feature for the writer to have included in the text? Explain your answer.

   ....

   ....

   (2 marks)

Spelling, Punctuation & Grammar Question

5. Underline the spelling mistake in each sentence.
   Then write the correct spelling on the line.

   a) Queen Sara held an enormous bankwet for her supporters. ....

   b) Numerous gards attended to shield her from any hazards. ....

   (2 marks)

Writing Question

6. a) The sentences below make up the first paragraph of an article written by somebody who took a trip to Borton Castle, but the sentences are in the wrong order. Number the sentences 1-4 to put them in the correct order.

   Throughout the show, our tour guide answered my questions easily. ☐

   Our tour began with a highly entertaining live jousting performance. ☐

   We congregated after the show, then proceeded to the next attraction. ☐

   Just as the performance started, our group managed to find our seats. ☐

   (1 mark)

   b) Use the information about Borton Castle on the previous page to write the next paragraph of the article. Structure your paragraph in a logical way, adding detail where appropriate.

   ....

   ....

   ....

   ....

   ....

   ....

   (3 marks)

   Score: ☐ /12

Summer Term: Workout 5

Warm up

1. What is meant by the term 'reported speech'?

   ....

   (1 mark)

Reading Questions

> So, Dad proposes his idea for Family Fun Day and we aren't exactly thrilled about it. I mean, a whole hour locked inside a room with no way out but to work together to escape? Sounds like a recipe for disaster if you ask me. But no one ever does ask me, do they? It's always, "Ayana, get in the car", "Ayana, sit in the middle". I'm always sitting in the middle.
>
> Anyway, we walk into the escape room and it is DARK. Dad starts with his usual speech about how we're a 'team', but my sisters are busy shrieking over the skeleton in the corner.
>
> Then we spot the coconut shy puzzle, and we're all invested now because the funfair is where the Family Fun Day tradition started. First, Dad topples one with ease, then I do the same. The skeleton cheers every time we hit one, and we're laughing, really laughing. One coconut falls, then another. More laughing. Okay, I think, maybe this isn't so bad.

2. a) A key theme of the extract is family relations. How is Ayana's relationship with her family presented in the first paragraph? Support your answer with evidence.

   ....

   ....

   (2 marks)

   b) How does Ayana's attitude towards spending time with her family change towards the end of the extract? Give evidence to support your answer.

   ....

   ....

   (2 marks)

3. Explain how you can tell that Ayana's family value spending time with each other.

   ....

   (1 mark)

Spelling, Punctuation & Grammar Question

4. Rewrite these examples of direct speech so they are punctuated correctly.

   a) can we have a clue the team asks

   ....

   b) Ayana shouts enter the code into the keypad

   ....

   c) look inside all the coat pockets Dad instructs

   ....

   (3 marks)

Writing Question

5. Choose one of the story prompts below, then write the story's opening paragraph. Make sure your opening uses descriptive language and grabs the reader's attention.

   | An escape room set in a vampire's lair | An escape room set in a tropical jungle | An escape room set on a pirate ship |

   ....

   ....

   ....

   ....

   ....

   ....

   ....

   (3 marks)

Score: /12

Summer Term: Workout 6

Warm up

1. Why might a writer use statistics in a report?

   ....
   (1 mark)

Reading Questions

Ever find yourself bored at home in the evening? Looking to fill your time with a creative, calming and enriching activity? Well, look no further.

Join our weekly knitting club 'Stitch in Time'. We're a friendly, close-knit bunch of crafting fanatics. We're always keen to welcome novice knitters to the group, so we provide all the resources and assistance required to get you happily 'hooked' on your wholesome new hobby!

With 7.3 million Brits already knitting their own hats and scarves, you too could have a new winter wardrobe in no time! So, what are you waiting for? Come along to the town hall every Thursday at 6 pm, and unravel the joys of knitting!

2. Why has the writer written this text?

   ....
   (1 mark)

3. What technique is used in the phrase: "happily 'hooked' on your wholesome new hobby"? Why do you think the writer uses this technique?

   ....

   ....
   (1 mark)

4. What tone does the writer use? Why do you think they chose to use this tone?

   ....

   ....
   (2 marks)

Spelling, Punctuation & Grammar Question

5. Fill in the gap in each sentence with the correct possessive pronoun to replace the words in brackets.

   a) Sue ran out of wool, so I lent her some of .... *(my wool)*.

   b) My brother broke my headphones, so he gave me .... *(my brother's)*.

   c) Other villages have parks, but .... *(our village)* has a swimming pool.

   (3 marks)

Writing Questions

6. Write a short paragraph informing the reader about your favourite hobby and explaining why you like it.

   ....
   ....
   ....
   ....
   (2 marks)

7. Write a paragraph advising the reader on how to find a new hobby. Use two features for writing to advise (e.g. second-person pronouns, a logical structure).

   ....
   ....
   ....
   ....
   (2 marks)

Score: ⬜ / 12

Summer Term: Workout 7

Warm up

1. Which of these words is a half-rhyme for 'storm'? Tick the correct option.

    swarm ☐   perform ☐   charm ☐   norm ☐

    (1 mark)

Reading Questions

> These are the roots that ground me,
> Securing my trunk to earth.
> This is the bark that acts as my cloak,
> Wrapped up like a newborn since birth.
>
> These are the leaves that shade you,
> And all those that nestle within,
> I serve as a shield in wind and in rain,
> For the ecosystem inside my skin.
>
> Yet, here come your giant machines,
> Greedy and eager to grind.
> You turn me to pulp and wear down my soil,
> Gambling the future of mankind.
>
> These are the roots that ground me,
> No longer secured to earth.
> You tore them up with no remorse,
> And stripped away all that I'm worth.

2. Tick the rhyme scheme used in the poem. Then explain the effect of this rhyme scheme in the first two stanzas.

    AABB ☐   ABBA ☐   ABCB ☐   ABAB ☐

    ....

    ....

    (2 marks)

3. a) What do you notice about the first two lines of the final stanza?

    ....

   b) What is the effect of this?

    ....

    ....

    (2 marks)

Spelling, Punctuation & Grammar Question

4. Circle the correct option to complete each sentence below.

   a) We would like to say **thankyou / thank you** for your generous donation.

   b) Deforestation is **infact / in fact** a real threat to our planet.

   c) If we're not careful, the rainforest could disappear **altogether / all together** .

   d) With your help, we can do **alot / a lot** to protect the rainforest.

   (4 marks)

Writing Question

5. a) Here is another line from the poem on page 62.
   Write the next line of the poem, using personification.

   > These are the branches that sway in the breeze,

   ....
   (1 mark)

   b) Here is another line from the poem.
   Write the line that comes after it, using a metaphor.

   > These are the blossoms that fall to the ground,

   ....
   (1 mark)

   c) This is another line from the poem.
   Write the next line, using a simile.

   > The future is precious and sacred,

   ....
   (1 mark)

   Score: / 12

Summer Term: Workout 8

Warm up

1. Circle the stage direction that could be used to make a character seem mysterious.

   | solemnly | wearily | frantically | slyly |

   (1 mark)

Reading Questions

The stage is in complete darkness. A single, white spotlight flashes on, illuminating a small table centre-stage with only a telephone on it. It lets out a shrill ringing sound, stops, then rings again. After several rings, **MRS. R** *enters. She stares at the telephone, then picks it up.*

MRS. R   Mrs. R speaking. Who is this? *(tapping her foot)* And what can I do for you?

There is a pause. **MRS. R** *adjusts the wide brim of the hat that covers her eyes as she listens.*

MRS. R   I see. Right. Very well. That much? *(pursing her lips)* And you're absolutely sure?

The spotlight above her dims slightly. A harsh piano tune gets slowly louder.

MRS. R   Good day to you too. *(ramming the telephone back into its receiver)* What an unbelievable farce! *(taking off her hat to reveal her furrowed brow)* It appears I find myself in quite the predicament...

2. How could an actor playing Mrs. R speak to show the phone call brings bad news?

   ....

   (1 mark)

3. What effect does the *"shrill ringing"* of the telephone have? How would the scene's atmosphere change if this sound was a pleasant tune instead?

   ....

   ....

   (2 marks)

4. The audience can only hear one side of the phone call. What is the effect of this?

   ....

   ....

   (1 mark)

Spelling, Punctuation & Grammar Question

5. Fill in the gap in each sentence using either 'its' or 'it's'.

   a) I phoned the vet to tell him that my cat got something stuck in .... paw.

   b) .... been a few weeks since I last spoke to my sister, so I'll call her.

   c) I want to phone my friend, but .... already midnight.

   (3 marks)

Writing Question

6. Fill in the gaps to show what the person on the other end of Mrs. R's phone call is saying. Give your new character a name, and use stage directions and their dialogue to make them seem rude.

   MRS. R   Mrs. R speaking. Who is this? *(tapping her foot)*

   ....

   MRS. R   And what can I do for you?

   ....

   ....

   MRS. R   I see. Right. Very well. That much?

   ....

   MRS. R   *(pursing her lips)* And you're absolutely sure?

   ....

   MRS. R   Good day to you too. *(ramming the telephone back into its receiver)*

   (4 marks)

Score: /12

Summer Term: Workout 9

Warm up

1. What tone is a diary entry most likely to have? Circle your answer.

   formal   complimentary   honest   advisory

   (1 mark)

Reading Questions

> Day 287, Langwell Sands (again)
>
> Another unsuccessful day out on the dunes. Possibly the least fruitful attempt yet. The conditions initially appeared promising, but my hope diminished after spending an hour scouring the deserted expanse of the bay, my gear heavy as lead, with little to show for it. Brilliant. It's not like this equipment cost me a month's salary or anything.
>
> To make matters worse, I scalded my tongue on my flask of hot tea when I paused for a drink at Pelican Point. The only comfort was the coastline — a velvety, golden duvet. Yet still, the shore taunts me. Still, its buried treasure does not reveal itself. Still, it refuses to share its secrets with me.... I must return tomorrow.

2. a) Tick the three techniques that are used in the text.

   simile ☐   onomatopoeia ☐   personification ☐   metaphor ☐

   b) Give an example of one of these techniques from the text.

   ....

   (2 marks)

3. Underline one example of sarcasm in the text. What effect does it have?

   ....

   ....

   (2 marks)

4. Why do you think the writer repeats "still" at the end of the extract?

   ....

   (1 mark)

Spelling, Punctuation & Grammar Question

5. Rewrite the sentences below in Standard English.

    a) I been looking for treasure like all day now.

    ....

    b) He was hoping for some coins, but he ain't found none.

    ....

    c) We was well happy when the machine started beeping.

    ....
    (3 marks)

Writing Question

6. Read this extract from the next entry of the diary on page 66.
    Rewrite the extract, correcting any spelling and grammar mistakes
    and replacing the underlined words with more interesting alternatives.

    > I went back, and this time I was determined to unveil something <u>good</u>. Equiped with my trusty metal detector, I ventured across the bay. However, their was one problem: someone else had beated me to it. Did he not know who's beach this was? It makes me <u>mad</u> just thinking about it.

    ....

    ....

    ....

    ....

    ....

    ....
    (3 marks)

Score: ☐ / 12

Summer Term: Workout 10

Warm up

1. Circle the words that you would be likely to use when comparing texts.

   contrarily   undoubtedly   conversely   likewise

   (1 mark)

Reading Questions

A We were delighted at the thought of seeing father's old home, and living among the haunts of his boyhood. He had talked so much to us about it that he had inspired us with some of his own deep-seated affection for it. We had a vague feeling that we, somehow, belonged there, in that cradle of our family, though we had never seen it.

An abridged extract from *The Story Girl* by L. M. Montgomery

B My stomach roars out in hunger as I traipse across the vast plain, restless and pleading for the comfort of shelter. I yearn for cosy sitting rooms and plush armchairs, downy pillows and a glowing fire. I blink, and before my eyes appears a brick-red house, momentarily igniting the hope buried deep inside of me. But the building vanishes, and I am alone again. So alone.

2. How do the writers of both texts present home as a place of safety? Explain your answer using evidence from each text.

   ....

   ....

   ....

   (2 marks)

3. What mood is created at the end of each text? Support your answer with evidence.

   ....

   ....

   ....

   (2 marks)

Spelling, Punctuation & Grammar Question

4. Circle the correct word to complete each sentence below.

   a) The garden is far **to / too / two** small for all my pets, I'm afraid.

   b) There are **to / too / two** spacious bedrooms on the second floor.

   c) I was dismayed **to / too / two** learn that the house had been sold.

   (3 marks)

Writing Question

5. Imagine that you have been asked to write a story about a character who is moving into an unusual house.

   a) Write a description of the house as your character first sees it.
      Use the first person and include figurative language to engage the reader.

   ....

   ....

   ....

   ....

   (2 marks)

   b) Write a paragraph about your character entering the house. Use language techniques and the paragraph's structure to create a specific atmosphere.

   ....

   ....

   ....

   ....

   ....

   (2 marks)

   Score: ☐ / 12

Summer Term: Workout 11

Warm up

1. Give an example of a type of text that might use a friendly tone.

   ....

   (1 mark)

Reading Questions

> Guess what? I managed to steal your favourite tennis couple, Ace and Annette Jones, for a chat about what's been going on in their lives both on and off the court...
>
> I first got the chance to chat to Ace. You Ace-inators know that he's been on outstanding form lately, dominating on both grass and clay. I was in awe of his swift serves during yesterday's final, and it was no surprise when victory was his.
>
> Ace, humble as ever, accepted his trophy gracefully before telling me, "This isn't the only thing I'm celebrating right now." I was rather baffled, until Annette, who secured the title in the Women's Final last week, joined us to celebrate. To my surprise, the couple shared with me the exciting news that they are expecting a baby in the new year! Looks like tennis has a future star in the making...

2. Who do you think is the writer's intended audience? Explain your answer using evidence from the text.

   ....

   ....

   (2 marks)

3. a) How does the writer create an informal tone?

   ....

   ....

   b) Why is this an effective tone for the writer's intended audience?

   ....

   ....

   (2 marks)

Spelling, Punctuation & Grammar Question

4. Circle the correct word to complete each sentence below.

   a) I haven't warmed up yet, so **lets / let's** do a few more laps of the track.

   b) After a run-up, she **lets / let's** go of the javelin and it soars through the air.

   c) I hope that she **lets / let's** us compete in the netball tournament next week.

   (3 marks)

Writing Question

5. Imagine that you have been asked to write an essay with the following title:
   'Competitive video gaming, known as eSports, should be included in the Olympics. How far do you agree?'

   a) In note form, write two points you could make to agree with the statement.

   • ....

   • ....

   (1 mark)

   b) In note form, write two points you could make to challenge the statement.

   • ....

   • ....

   (1 mark)

   c) Write a conclusion to the essay, in which you say how far you agree with the statement and explain your reasoning.

   ....

   ....

   ....

   ....

   ....

   (2 marks)

   Score: ☐ /12

Summer Term: Workout 12

Warm up

1. Give two things you could look at when analysing a poem's structure.

   ....
   (1 mark)

Reading Questions

> Some day, when trees have shed their leaves
>   And against the morning's white
> The shivering birds beneath the eaves*
>   Have sheltered for the night,
> We'll turn our faces southward, love,
>   Toward the summer isle
> Where bamboos spire the shafted grove
>   And wide-mouthed orchids smile.
>
> And we will seek the quiet hill
>   Where towers the cotton tree,
> And leaps the laughing crystal rill**,
>   And works the droning bee.
> And we will build a cottage there
>   Beside an open glade,
> With black-ribbed blue-bells blowing near,
>   And ferns that never fade.

*eaves — *the edges of a roof*   **rill — *a small stream*

**'After the Winter'
by Claude McKay**

2. Write down an example of personification from the poem.
   What does it suggest about the narrator's attitude towards summer?

   ....

   ....
   (2 marks)

3. What is the effect of using first-person narration in the poem?

   ....

   ....
   (1 mark)

4. What is the effect of using the future tense in the poem?

   ....

   ....
   (1 mark)

Spelling, Punctuation & Grammar Question

5. Fill in the gap in each of these lines from 'After the Winter' with the simple past tense form of the verb in brackets.

   And we .... the quiet hill *(to seek)*

   Where .... the cotton tree, *(to tower)*

   And .... the laughing crystal rill, *(to leap)*

   And .... the droning bee. *(to work)*

   (2 marks)

Writing Question

6. Imagine you are writing a poem about one of the topics below.

   | a forest | night-time | a cottage | birds | flowers |

   a) What mood would you try to create in your poem?

   ....
   (1 mark)

   b) Write down a simile or metaphor that you could use to help create this mood.

   ....
   (1 mark)

   c) Write the opening stanza of a poem about your chosen topic, using your answers to parts a) and b) to help you. Give your stanza a regular rhyme scheme.

   ....

   ....

   ....

   ....
   (3 marks)

Score: /12

Answers

Autumn Term

Workout 1 — pages 2-3

1. a mystery novel *(1 mark)*

2. a) Text A — E.g. a textbook
      Text B — E.g. an advert
      (1 mark)
   b) E.g. It uses techniques like exaggeration and second-person pronouns to persuade the reader to use the scooters. *(1 mark)*

3. a) E.g. "plasters were being mass-produced by 1924"
   b) E.g. "It's the best mode of supermarket transport out there!"
      (1 mark for each)

4. a) <u>Their</u> newest invention is the flying car.
   b) <u>They're</u> calling it the best thing since sliced bread.
   c) <u>There</u> may well be flying carpets soon too.
      (1 mark for each)

5. Any sensible answer that details a more specific quote from Akeem. E.g. Akeem commented, "I was incredibly scared at first, but the magnificence of the volcano took my breath away". *(1 mark)*

6. Any three sensible points *(1 mark for each)*

Workout 2 — pages 4-5

1. based on evidence *(1 mark)*

2. E.g. The text says that Wren has "won big". *(1 mark)*

3. a) indifferent
   b) "Warbler initially paid no notice to the ticket"
      (1 mark)

4. E.g. The text says that "the eyes of the Trust's founder lit up". *(1 mark)*

5. a) Many species of birds are at risk due to climate <u>change's</u> impact on the world.
   b) A study was done by <u>Wren's</u> colleagues about which owls face the most threats.
   c) The <u>study's</u> results show snowy owls will suffer from changes to their habitat.
      (1 mark for each)

6. Any sensible plan
   (1 mark for an introduction, 1 mark for each point, 1 mark for a conclusion)

Workout 3 — pages 6-7

1. E.g. How the beats are arranged within a line. *(1 mark)*

2. a) True
   b) True
      (1 mark for each)

3. E.g. It gives the poem a faster pace, creating the sense that the storm isn't going to stop. *(1 mark)*

4. E.g. It reflects that bad weather doesn't last. This creates a calm atmosphere, as peace has been restored. *(1 mark for writing why the stanza is repeated, 1 mark for explaining the effect)*

5. I trudged home alone <u>through</u> the storm, / <u>Though</u> I didn't feel too forlorn. / To my house I retired, / Where my roaring fire, / Did a <u>thorough</u> job of keeping me warm.
   (1 mark for each)

6. Any haiku that addresses the prompt *(1 mark for each line with the correct number of syllables)*

Workout 4 — pages 8-9

1. E.g. The general atmosphere of a text. *(1 mark)*

2. E.g. The mood is suspenseful and tense. *(1 mark)*

3. E.g. It gives the reader the sense that the narrator is overwhelmed by criticism. *(1 mark)*

4. E.g. Hopeful because the narrator has started feeling like there might be a positive outcome. *(1 mark for writing how it makes you feel, 1 mark for a sensible explanation)*

5. a) elves
   b) thieves
   c) lives
      (1 mark for each)

6. a) Any sensible answer
      (1 mark for naming a mood, 1 mark for explaining how that mood could be created)
   b) Any sensible answer
      (1 mark for each feature of the character's personality that is described)

Workout 5 — pages 10-11

1. E.g. To make your argument more convincing. *(1 mark)*

2. a) critical
   b) E.g. The writer uses negative language and lists everything that was wrong with their dining experience.
      (1 mark for each)

3. E.g. Yes. It is a letter of complaint, so a critical tone is appropriate, as the writer wants to express their dissatisfaction with their experience. *(1 mark)*

4. a) On Friday_∧ we have a reservation for dinner at the local pub.
   b) At the back of the café_∧ there is a grand piano that diners can play.
   c) Without warning_∧ the critic stood up and stormed out of the eatery.
      (1 mark for each)

5. Any sensible answer *(1 mark for using alliteration, 1 mark for using a rhetorical question, 1 mark for using a list of three)*

6. Any sensible answer *(1 mark for using emotive language, 1 mark for using at least one fact)*

Answers

Workout 6 — pages 12-13

1. lonely *(1 mark)*

2. E.g. It suggests that their petals look like neat, perfectly folded pieces of paper. *(1 mark)*

3. E.g. The other bees have taken all their pollen. *(1 mark)*

4. E.g. The female bee signals to the male bee that she has found one last bit of nectar for them to share. *(1 mark for explaining what happens, 1 mark for using your own words)*

5. a) The beekeeper put the hive <u>nearby</u> so that he could talk to his bees <u>often</u>.
   b) The bee flew <u>swiftly</u> to the flower and landed <u>softly</u> on the yellow petal.
   c) The honey that I bought at the market is <u>quite</u> sweet and <u>really</u> fragrant.
   (1 mark for each correct sentence)

6. Any sensible answer *(1 mark for each line that matches the rhythm of the first pair of lines)*

7. Any sensible answer *(1 mark for using descriptive language, 1 mark for matching the rhythm of the first pair of lines)*

Workout 7 — pages 14-15

1. the main character *(1 mark)*

2. a) E.g. Nervous. He is "biting his lip" and "glancing around". *(1 mark for naming a feeling, 1 mark for giving evidence)*
   b) E.g. They aren't allowed in the library at night. *(1 mark)*

3. A ghost.
   E.g. The boy "materialises" while Sabina and Fergus are looking for a book about ghouls, which suggests that he is supernatural.
   (1 mark for writing what the boy is, 1 mark for an explanation that uses evidence from the text)

4. a) We <u>are</u> looking for books about witches.
   b) My neighbour claims that <u>our</u> house is haunted.
   c) <u>Our</u> class is going ghost hunting next weekend.
   (1 mark for each)

5. Any sensible play script that uses the plan to continue the story *(1 mark for adding detail to each point, 1 mark for using stage directions, 1 mark for using dialogue)*

Workout 8 — pages 16-17

1. You should have ticked: profession, session *(1 mark)*

2. a) Text A
   b) E.g. The writer hopes to see "familiar faces", which suggests the bakery has a community of people close by that regularly come in.
   (1 mark for each)

3. a) E.g. People who have an interest in high-quality bread.
   b) E.g. The text says that customers can buy "the finest loaves that you've always wanted to try", which suggests it's aimed at people who care about bread.
   (1 mark for each)

4. Dubbed 'pastry magi<u>cian</u>', Monsieur Boulangerie has made quite the impre<u>ssion</u> due to his objec<u>tion</u> to tradi<u>tion</u>. "I am a baking techni<u>cian</u>! My mi<u>ssion</u> is to find new flavours!" he insists.
   (1 mark for every 2 correct)

5. a) Any sensible slogan *(1 mark)*
   b) Any sensible final sentence that includes an opinion *(1 mark)*
   c) Any sensible advert about the new dessert *(1 mark for using emotive language, 1 mark for using a list of three)*

Workout 9 — pages 18-19

1. E.g. To put an idea into your own words. *(1 mark)*

2. a) E.g. He feels panicked and anxious.
   b) E.g. He has "trembling hands".
   (1 mark for each)

3. E.g. He needs to get food for himself and his grandma so they don't starve. *(1 mark)*

4. E.g. They have a close relationship and depend on each other. *(1 mark)*

5. You should have underlined: brave, unwanted, countless
   You should have circled: Soon, fast, desperately
   (1 mark for every 2 correct)

6. 1 — Arlo was brought out of his thoughts by the sound of rustling in the trees.
   2 — He crouched down behind a bush, hearing a raspy voice begin to speak.
   3 — "Keep an eye out for fugitives — there's always some lurking in the forest."
   4 — "They'll find it mightily difficult to hide from me," another voice replied.
   (1 mark for all)

7. Any sensible plan *(1 mark for every 2 plot points, 1 mark for structuring the story so the atmosphere becomes more tense)*

Answers

Workout 10 — pages 20-21

1. to persuade *(1 mark)*

2. **a)** to advise — B
   to argue — C
   to inform — A
   (1 mark for all)
   b) E.g. Facts
   E.g. Second-person pronouns
   (1 mark)
   c) E.g. A rhetorical question. It encourages the reader to agree that the given risks of using smartphones are bad enough without listing more. *(1 mark for identifying a feature, 1 mark for explaining why it suits the text's purpose)*

3. **a)** There is one huge reason why I'm afraid of robots<u>:</u> sci-fi films.
   b) I need two things<u>:</u> a computer keyboard and a monitor.
   c) I slammed the laptop shut<u>:</u> I had finally finished my homework.
   (1 mark for each)

4. **a)** Any sensible points in favour of the prompt *(1 mark)*
   b) Any sensible points against the prompt *(1 mark)*
   c) Any sensible paragraph based on one of your points *(1 mark for a clear structure, 1 mark for adding detail)*

Workout 11 — pages 22-23

1. E.g. Where something is in relation to something else. *(1 mark)*

2. **a)** E.g. She couldn't achieve her dreams on the island, but she could in the city.
   b) "Chasing goals and hopes and dreams, / That don't grow on that tiny isle."
   (1 mark for each)

3. The woman wonders whether she should have left the island. *(1 mark)*

4. Living <u>on</u> an island is phenomenal. People who don't live <u>near</u> the sea rarely see the ocean, but I live <u>beside</u> it, so the sight is a familiar one. Every day, I head <u>to</u> the beach <u>with</u> my dog and witness the sun emerging <u>over</u> the horizon. The sand sinks <u>between</u> my toes as the waves lap <u>at</u> the shore. *(1 mark for every 2 prepositions)*

5. Any sensible lines that use five syllables *(1 mark for each line)*

Workout 12 — pages 24-25

1. E.g. bang, crash, pop *(1 mark)*

2. oxymoron *(1 mark)*

3. E.g. "Zuri's heart was a pounding drum" suggests that Zuri is full of adrenaline, as her heart is beating loudly. *(1 mark)*

4. **a)** E.g. It gives the sense that the action is happening quickly.
   b) Any two sensible answers, e.g. personification, alliteration, onomatopoeia, simile, metaphor, imagery.
   (1 mark for each)

5. **a)** phrase
   b) clause
   c) phrase
   (1 mark for each)

6. **a)** E.g. The stars sparkled as dazzlingly as diamonds.
   b) E.g. Fear passed across the alien's face like a dark cloud.
   (1 mark for each)

7. **a)** Any sensible sentence that uses a metaphor
   b) Any sensible sentence that uses hyperbole
   (1 mark for each)

Spring Term

Workout 1 — pages 26-27

1. E.g. columns of text *(1 mark)*

2. E.g. Highlighting that the book is a bestseller makes it more appealing to buyers. *(1 mark)*

3. E.g. The first paragraph uses rhetorical questions to capture the reader's attention, then the second paragraph gives a solution to the questions. *(1 mark)*

4. E.g. *The Help Journal* gave the book more stars and called it the "BEST" self-help book, so the writer would want readers to see the better review first. *(1 mark for explaining why this review comes first, 1 mark for using evidence from the text)*

5. **a)** The new album <u>by</u> Melody Funk is the best album of the year.
   b) I'm saving up to <u>buy</u> tickets to see my favourite singer live.
   c) Rex left to go on tour with his band and he didn't even say <u>bye</u>.
   (1 mark for each)

6. The article says the album has a "fairylike spirit". This, along with its "angelic harmonies", creates a whimsical feel. *(1 mark for each correct quote)*

7. **a)** E.g. They are appearing "in city centres all over the country".
   b) E.g. They want to "get the nation dancing".
   (1 mark for each)

Workout 2 — pages 28-29

1. E.g. caring, active and responsible *(1 mark for three traits)*

2. **a)** E.g. A friendly, sociable person.
   b) E.g. She greets "any unsuspecting person" she comes across.
   (1 mark for each)

3. E.g. He is a pessimistic person and doesn't appreciate Miss Fenwick's enthusiasm. *(1 mark)*

Answers

4. E.g. Miss Fenwick is fond of Mr Halpert. She smiles "softly" when she sees him, which suggests she feels affectionate towards him. *(1 mark for writing how you think Miss Fenwick feels, 1 mark for explaining why)*

5. a) That cottage, the home of Mr. Halpert, is over 300 years old.
   b) Miss Fenwick, beaming from ear to ear, commended its beauty.
   c) Her impatient poodle, quick to get bored, tugged on its lead.
   (1 mark for each)

6. Any sensible sentences *(1 mark for each sentence)*

Workout 3 — pages 30-31

1. E.g. To look quickly over a text for specific information. *(1 mark)*

2. a) captivated
   b) E.g. The writer says that "few other places have enthralled me as much", which suggests they were mesmerised by the area.
   (1 mark for each)

3. E.g. They got to explore the island and see lots of pretty spots, but they were very hot and didn't have time to swim in the caves to cool down. *(1 mark for summarising the positives, 1 mark for summarising the negatives)*

4. a) Ella's grandad <u>doesn't</u> speak Greek at home, so she <u>doesn't</u> know any.
   b) Why <u>don't</u> we go to Corfu instead? The journey <u>doesn't</u> take as long.
   (1 mark for each correct sentence)

5. Any sensible redraft. E.g. The food in Greece is mouth-watering; it's my favourite aspect of the country. There are countless restaurants to visit, each one serving a wonderful selection of traditional Greek dishes. *(1 mark for using interesting vocabulary, 1 mark for using interesting sentence structures)*

6. I have found <u>Athens</u> in particular to be a simply breathtaking city, brimming with <u>fascinating</u> museums, magnificent <u>buildings</u> and rich culture. The Parthenon is just as you see it in pictures; it was <u>an</u> absolute treat to visit this <u>ancient</u> structure. I could <u>have</u> looked at it for ages, but I had to meet up with my friend for dinner. *(1 mark for every 2 correct)*

Workout 4 — pages 32-33

1. E.g. A form of poetry that doesn't have a regular rhyme or rhythm. *(1 mark)*

2. E.g. They are worried they are less valuable now that they are older. *(1 mark)*

3. E.g. Language about loss, such as the tree having "lost its leaves", creates a sense that ageing is something to be mourned. *(1 mark)*

4. E.g. Winter imagery, such as wrinkles spreading "like cracks on ice" creates the sense that ageing, like winter, is a harsh season of someone's life. *(1 mark for an idea, 1 mark for explaining it)*

5. a) tick
   b) cross
   c) cross
   d) tick
   (1 mark for each)

6. Any sensible rhyming couplets that address the prompt *(1 mark for each couplet)*

Workout 5 — pages 34-35

1. E.g. peaceful *(1 mark)*

2. E.g. "They looked straight over her, refusing to acknowledge an outsider." *(1 mark)*

3. a) unwelcoming
   b) E.g. Annie hoped for a smile from the people in the city, but the smile "never came".
   (1 mark for each)

4. E.g. The narrator says that the people in the city have "urgency coursing through their veins", which suggests they are always in a rush. *(1 mark)*

5. a) self-control
   b) ex-mayor
   c) long-term
   (1 mark for each)

6. Any sensible answer. E.g. Dilapidated buildings and piercing silence surrounded me. I ventured down a forgotten alleyway, passing boarded-up windows and imagining the shadows of strangers at every turn. *(1 mark for rewriting the description so it is appropriate for a story set in an abandoned city, 1 mark for using language that creates an eerie atmosphere)*

7. Any sensible answer *(1 mark for describing a setting for one of the story titles, 1 mark for creating a specific atmosphere)*

Workout 6 — pages 36-37

1. E.g. Simple, clear language and second-person narration. *(1 mark for two features)*

2. E.g. The job of a nurse. The writer talks about working "on the wards", "Helping the doctors" and having "patients", which suggests they work in a medical setting. *(1 mark for identifying the job and explaining how you can tell)*

3. E.g. They are studious and wanted to be prepared for their job. *(1 mark)*

4. E.g. The writer says they were "nearly drowning" on their first day, which suggests that they struggled initially. *(1 mark for describing how the writer initially managed their job, 1 mark for explaining your answer)*

5. a) F
   b) I
   c) I
   (1 mark for each)

Answers

6. a) Any sensible paragraph that introduces the speech *(1 mark for including a fact about being a paramedic)*
    b) Any sensible answer *(1 mark for explaining one trait)*

7. Any sensible answer *(1 mark for using second-person pronouns, 1 mark for using a reassuring tone)*

Workout 7 — pages 38-39

1. E.g. A way of describing something by saying it is like something else. *(1 mark)*

2. E.g. "a laughter cold as the frost" *(1 mark)*

3. a) personification
    b) E.g. It creates the sense that the forest is an unfriendly place. *(1 mark for each)*

4. E.g. The adjective "ominous" suggests that there is a threat of danger. The forest's laughter is described as "terrible", which suggests that the forest is full of evil. *(1 mark for each adjective that is explained)*

5. a) E.g. The river was cold but the wolf swam across anyway.
    b) E.g. I don't want to go outside for there is a snowstorm. *(1 mark for each)*

6. The snow persisted all night, never lessening or pausing. Little by little, the track was covered over. When we woke up, Alia and I saw that the track had become too indistinct to follow, so we wouldn't be able to reach the town. *(1 mark for every 3 corrections)*

7. Any sensible answer.
    E.g. The explorer woke with a start. Glancing around, he immediately began to panic. The world was a blank canvas, utterly covered in snow, and he was entirely unsure as to the direction he should take. *(1 mark for using more interesting vocabulary, 1 mark for using more interesting sentence structures)*

Workout 8 — pages 40-41

1. E.g. An argument that opposes another argument. *(1 mark)*

2. In this awfully good thriller — oxymoron
    awards will be knocking at Arjun's door — personification *(1 mark for each)*

3. E.g. It creates suspense, as it leaves the reader wondering if Arjun will ever make a mistake. *(1 mark)*

4. E.g. "eye-popping, blood-rushing and head-spinning".
    This emphasises that the film is exciting. *(1 mark for an example, 1 mark for explaining its effect)*

5. a) The cinema is handing out free buckets of popcorn (the sweet variety) to encourage passersby to come in and buy a ticket.
    b) Flick Clément (who is a famous actor) is best known for her portrayal of a young mathematician in *The Power of 10*.
    (1 mark for each)

6. a) Any sensible answers *(1 mark for 2 points that support the statement)*
    b) Any sensible answers *(1 mark for 2 points that challenge the statement)*
    c) Any sensible paragraph based on one of your points *(1 mark for a clear structure, 1 mark for adding detail)*

Workout 9 — pages 42-43

1. You should have underlined: mighty, steep, stunning *(1 mark for all)*

2. A volcano *(1 mark)*

3. E.g. The volcano seems powerful and all-knowing compared to the reader. *(1 mark)*

4. E.g. The line "But here I stand, unchanging" creates a proud tone, while the line "Dormant I no longer lie!" creates a lively tone. *(1 mark for describing the tone of each line)*

5. a) We need three things in our survival kit: water, food and medicine.
    b) Jonny climbed all the way to the top; Ravinder stayed at the bottom.
    (1 mark for each)

6. Any sensible adjectives.
    E.g. The scorching sun beats down
    Upon the parched earth below.
    A vast space, lifeless and void,
    The wind's mournful sigh the only sound.
    (1 mark for every 2 adjectives)

7. Any sensible four-line poem about a cave *(1 mark for using the future tense, 1 mark for using interesting adjectives, 1 mark for using first-person narration)*

Workout 10 — pages 44-45

1. E.g. To provide a backstory for a character. *(1 mark)*

2. E.g. He is only pretending to care about the victim for the interview. *(1 mark)*

3. E.g. This creates suspense, as the reader gradually pieces the events together just like the detective did. *(1 mark)*

Answers

4. E.g. It leaves the reader on a cliffhanger, as it implies that some characters may be lying about not being involved with the murder. *(1 mark for identifying the effect, 1 mark for explaining your answer)*

5. Sutcliffe Manor's cook, Cassie Role, keeps the <u>recipe</u> for her famous 'Death by Chocolate' cake <u>concealed</u>. I <u>recently</u> had a slice — it truly is a killer dessert! *(1 mark for each word)*

6. E.g. I have decided that tomorrow shall be the day. I have <u>dealt</u> with her <u>irritating</u> demands for far too long. She has <u>rejected</u> every dish I serve. "It could use a pinch of salt<u>,"</u> she announces <u>smugly</u>. Well, I refuse to <u>accept</u> this impolite behaviour. I will strike when everyone is drowsy from all the food and the port. Yes, <u>it's</u> going to be <u>splendid</u>.
(1 mark for replacing both smudges with descriptive words, 1 mark for every 2 mistakes corrected)

Workout 11 — pages 46-47

1. E.g. To make the reader sympathise with your opinion. *(1 mark)*

2. hyperbole (exaggeration) *(1 mark)*

3. E.g. The tone of Text A is confident, as it boasts about the clothes on offer. Text B, however, has a critical tone, as the writer is unhappy with their purchase. *(1 mark)*

4. E.g. In Text A, second-person narration helps the reader to imagine themselves wearing the gowns. In Text B, it makes the letter feel more personal, as the shop owner is addressed directly. *(1 mark for explaining the effect of second-person narration in each text)*

5. a) Jim — my friend from school — knitted me a scarf for my birthday.
   b) The two shopkeepers — Layla and Kioshi — always get to work early.
   c) Midori lost her favourite piece of jewellery — her necklace — yesterday.
   (1 mark for each correct sentence)

6. Any sensible answer.
   E.g. We sell a wide range of beautiful jewellery, as well as a stunning collection of watches. All our items are priced very reasonably and you will be sure to find the perfect piece in our shop.
   (1 mark for each sentence that is rewritten using persuasive language)

7. Any sensible answer *(1 mark for a paragraph that argues in favour of shopping online, 1 mark for using techniques suitable for a text that is written to argue)*

Workout 12 — pages 48-49

1. acts, scenes *(1 mark)*

2. E.g. He knows that the robbery has failed and that Arnie will be angry. *(1 mark)*

3. E.g. He thinks Bob is unreliable. Arnie remarks that it isn't "a surprise" when Bob disappears. *(1 mark for giving an opinion, 1 mark for using evidence from the text)*

4. E.g. Bob brings "*doves*" instead of "*gloves*". This misunderstanding creates humour, as Arnie would be unlikely to want doves for a robbery. *(1 mark for making a point about how the writer creates humour, 1 mark for explaining your answer using evidence from the text)*

5. had, messed, worrying, caught, told, left *(1 mark for every 2 correct)*

6. E.g. The intruder is presented as menacing. There is a "startling creaking sound" as they walk, which creates a tense atmosphere. The narrator, however, is portrayed as nervous. They quickly "dart" away to hide and "goosebumps prickle along" their arms, which suggests they are panicked. *(1 mark for each correct quote)*

Summer Term

Workout 1 — pages 50-51

1. a job application — F
   a message to a friend — I
   a history essay — F
   a postcard — I
   (1 mark for all)

2. E.g. To encourage the reader to think about trying roast potatoes for themselves. *(1 mark)*

3. E.g. The writer uses sensory language such as "crispy" and "fluffy" to make roast potatoes seem particularly tasty. *(1 mark for using evidence to explain how the writer uses sensory language, 1 mark for explaining the effect of this)*

4. E.g. It makes the text less believable. The writer will benefit from people buying their roast potatoes, so they are probably exaggerating how good roast potatoes are. *(1 mark for writing what effect this information has on your opinion of the text, 1 mark for explaining why)*

5. happiness, copying, wheezily, envious *(1 mark for every 2 correct)*

Answers

6. Any sensible answer.
   E.g. Hi Melody,
   I just wanted to tell you that I totally agree with this article I read recently about how great roast potatoes are. I think roasties go amazingly well with most meals. When I eat out, I make a giant fuss if my roast potatoes aren't very nice — that's how strongly I feel about them.
   See you around,
   Edward
   (1 mark for rewriting each of the three sentences using informal language, 1 mark for using an informal greeting and sign-off)

Workout 2 — pages 52-53

1. False *(1 mark)*

2. a) E.g. It suggests that nature is cruel to the narrator and wants to cause them pain. *(1 mark)*
   b) E.g. "As water bellows". This makes the water seem powerful and intimidating.
   (1 mark for giving an example of personification, 1 mark for explaining its effect)

3. E.g. It emphasises that humans can't defeat nature, as nature is much more powerful. *(1 mark)*

4. a) <u>Who's</u> going out on the boat today?
   b) I'm not sure <u>whose</u> oar this is.
   c) I need to know <u>who's</u> rowed before.
   (1 mark for each)

5. Any sensible lines that use one colour each *(1 mark for each line that uses at least one language technique)*

6. Any sensible four-line poem *(1 mark for using one language technique, or 2 marks for using two or more language techniques)*

Workout 3 — pages 54-55

1. E.g. It explains how events at the time may have influenced the writer. *(1 mark)*

2. E.g. "I have no pleasure in talking to undutiful children." *(1 mark)*

3. E.g. Mrs. Bennet does not have the means to support Lizzy, which suggests she relies on her husband for financial support. *(1 mark)*

4. E.g. The extract suggests that women were expected to marry, whether they wanted to or not, as shown by Mrs. Bennet's complaint that Lizzy keeps "refusing every offer of marriage". *(1 mark for writing what the extract suggests about marriage, 1 mark for explaining your answer using evidence)*

5. a) ambi<u>tious</u>
   b) cau<u>tious</u>
   c) pre<u>cious</u>
   (1 mark for each)

6. Any sensible answer *(1 mark for coming up with a sensible old-fashioned setting, 1 mark for thinking of a main character, 1 mark for describing the setting and main character using descriptive language)*

Workout 4 — pages 56-57

1. what type of text it is *(1 mark)*

2. E.g. To organise the information more clearly. *(1 mark)*

3. E.g. The font size is small, which means that the information in the box could easily be missed.
   (1 mark for writing a layout feature that makes the box ineffective, 1 mark for explaining why)

4. E.g. Yes. The image shows what the Great Tower looks like, which will help visitors recognise the tower when they see it. *(1 mark for giving an opinion, 1 mark for explaining your opinion)*

5. a) banquet
   b) guards
   (1 mark for each)

6. a) 1 — Our tour began with a highly entertaining live jousting performance.
   2 — Just as the performance started, our group managed to find our seats.
   3 — Throughout the show, our tour guide answered my questions easily.
   4 — We congregated after the show, then proceeded to the next attraction.
   (1 mark for all)
   b) Any sensible answer
   (1 mark for using the information given about Borton Castle, 1 mark for structuring your paragraph in a logical way, 1 mark for adding detail)

Workout 5 — pages 58-59

1. E.g. Describing what someone said without quoting them directly. *(1 mark)*

2. a) She feels like her opinions are overlooked by her family, as she is "always sitting in the middle" to suit them.
   (1 mark for describing how the relationship is presented, 1 mark for giving evidence)
   b) She starts to enjoy their company as they are "laughing" with each other, so she decides that maybe the day "isn't so bad" after all.
   (1 mark for describing how her attitude changes, 1 mark for giving evidence)

3. E.g. They have a family tradition where they do activities together. *(1 mark)*

4. a) "<u>C</u>an we have a clue<u>?</u>" the team asks<u>.</u>
   b) Ayana shouts<u>,</u> "<u>E</u>nter the code into the keypad!"
   c) "<u>L</u>ook inside all the coat pockets<u>,</u>" Dad instructs<u>.</u>
   (1 mark for each)

Answers

5. Any sensible answer *(1 mark for addressing the prompt, 1 mark for including descriptive language, 1 mark for grabbing the reader's attention)*

Workout 6 — pages 60-61

1. E.g. To support their points by providing evidence. *(1 mark)*
2. E.g. To persuade people to join their knitting club. *(1 mark)*
3. Alliteration.
    E.g. To make the advert memorable and therefore more persuasive.
    (1 mark for identifying the technique and explaining why it is used)
4. E.g. The writer uses a friendly tone to appeal to the reader and appear welcoming and approachable.
    (1 mark for identifying the tone, 1 mark for explaining why the writer chose to use it)
5. a) Sue ran out of wool, so I lent her some of <u>mine</u>.
    b) My brother broke my headphones, so he gave me <u>his</u>.
    c) Other villages have parks, but <u>ours</u> has a swimming pool.
    (1 mark for each)
6. Any sensible answer
    (1 mark for informing the reader about your favourite hobby, 1 mark for explaining why you like it)
7. Any sensible answer
    (1 mark for each feature that is suitable for writing to advise)

Workout 7 — pages 62-63

1. charm *(1 mark)*
2. ABCB
    E.g. The steady rhythm reflects how constant and reliable nature is.
    (1 mark for identifying the rhyme scheme, 1 mark for explaining its effect)
3. a) E.g. These lines were used to start the poem, but the second line has been altered.
    b) This emphasises how upsetting it is for the tree's life to end.
    (1 mark for each)
4. a) We would like to say <u>thank you</u> for your generous donation.
    b) Deforestation is <u>in fact</u> a real threat to our planet.
    c) If we're not careful, the rainforest could disappear <u>altogether</u>.
    d) With your help, we can do <u>a lot</u> to protect the rainforest.
    (1 mark for each)
5. a) E.g. They nod at those passing by.
    b) E.g. They are stars falling to Earth.
    c) E.g. As delicate as a cloud.
    (1 mark for each)

Workout 8 — pages 64-65

1. slyly *(1 mark)*
2. E.g. With a raised and panicked voice. *(1 mark)*
3. E.g. It builds tension around the phone call. A pleasant tune would make the atmosphere less threatening. *(1 mark for explaining the effect, 1 mark for explaining how the atmosphere would change)*
4. E.g. It creates intrigue, as the topic of conversation seems mysterious. *(1 mark)*
5. a) I phoned the vet to tell him that my cat got something stuck in <u>its</u> paw.
    b) <u>It's</u> been a few weeks since I last spoke to my sister, so I'll call her.
    c) I want to phone my friend, but <u>it's</u> already midnight.
    (1 mark for each)
6. Any sensible answers *(1 mark for every 2 plausible responses, 1 mark for using stage directions to make the character seem rude, 1 mark for using dialogue to make the character seem rude)*

Workout 9 — pages 66-67

1. honest *(1 mark)*
2. a) You should have ticked: simile, personification, metaphor
    b) E.g. "heavy as lead"
    (1 mark for each)
3. E.g. "It's not like this equipment cost me a months salary or anything." This suggests the narrator is frustrated because he has invested a lot of money and has nothing to show for it. *(1 mark for underlining an example of sarcasm, 1 mark for explaining its effect)*
4. E.g. It emphasises that the narrator has repeatedly had no success, despite their efforts. *(1 mark)*
5. a) E.g. I have been looking for treasure all day now.
    b) E.g. He was hoping for some coins, but he hasn't found any.
    c) E.g. We were very happy when the machine started beeping.
    (1 mark for each sentence)
6. E.g. I went back, and this time I was determined to unveil something <u>extraordinary</u>. <u>Equipped</u> with my trusty metal detector, I ventured across the bay. However, <u>there</u> was one problem: someone else had <u>beaten</u> me to it. Did he not know <u>whose</u> beach this was? It makes me <u>livid</u> just thinking about it.
    (1 mark for every 2 mistakes corrected, 1 mark for replacing both of the underlined words with more interesting alternatives)

Answers

Workout 10 — pages 68-69

1. You should have circled: contrarily, conversely, likewise *(1 mark for all)*

2. E.g. In Text A, the narrator describes home as a "cradle", and in Text B, the narrator longs for the "comfort of shelter" that a home provides. Both texts therefore show that home is a place that brings comfort and safety. *(1 mark for explaining how home is presented as a place of safety in both texts, 1 mark for using evidence from both texts)*

3. E.g. In Text A, the narrator feels they "belonged" in the house before they saw it, which creates a hopeful mood. In Text B, the narrator realises they are "So alone", which creates a despairing mood. *(1 mark for explaining the mood created at the end of both texts, 1 mark for using evidence from both texts)*

4. a) The garden is far <u>too</u> small for all my pets, I'm afraid.
   b) There are <u>two</u> spacious bedrooms on the second floor.
   c) I was dismayed <u>to</u> learn that the house had been sold.
   (1 mark for each)

5. a) Any sensible answer *(1 mark for using the first person, 1 mark for using figurative language)*
   b) Any sensible answer *(1 mark for using at least 2 language techniques to create a specific atmosphere, 1 mark for using the paragraph's structure to create a specific atmosphere)*

Workout 11 — pages 70-71

1. E.g. a letter to a friend *(1 mark)*

2. E.g. Fans of Ace and Annette Jones. The text refers to "your favourite tennis couple". *(1 mark for naming the audience, 1 mark for explaining your answer using evidence)*

3. a) E.g. By using conversational language such as "chat" and "Guess what?"
   b) E.g. It makes Ace and Annette seem as though they are the reader's friends, which makes them more easy to relate to.
   (1 mark for each)

4. a) I haven't warmed up yet, so <u>let's</u> do a few more laps of the track.
   b) After a run-up, she <u>lets</u> go of the javelin and it soars through the air.
   c) I hope that she <u>lets</u> us compete in the netball tournament next week.
   (1 mark for each)

5. a) Any sensible answers *(1 mark for 2 points that agree with the statement)*
   b) Any sensible answers *(1 mark for 2 points that challenge the statement)*
   c) Any sensible conclusion *(1 mark for saying how far you agree with the statement, 1 mark for explaining your reasoning)*

Workout 12 — pages 72-73

1. Any sensible answers. E.g. Line length and rhyme scheme. *(1 mark)*

2. E.g. "wide-mouthed orchids smile". It suggests that the narrator considers summer to be a joyful and pleasant time. *(1 mark for identifying an example of personification, 1 mark for explaining what it suggests)*

3. E.g. It makes the poem feel more personal and helps the reader to empathise with the narrator's dream of the future. *(1 mark)*

4. E.g. It makes the poem feel more hopeful, suggesting that the narrator is looking forward to what's to come. *(1 mark)*

5. And we <u>sought</u> the quiet hill
   Where <u>towered</u> the cotton tree,
   And <u>leapt</u> the laughing crystal rill,
   And <u>worked</u> the droning bee.
   (1 mark for every 2 correct)

6. a) Any sensible answer. E.g. peaceful *(1 mark)*
   b) Any sensible answer. E.g. "The sparrow glides downwards like a paper plane" *(1 mark)*
   c) Any sensible answer *(1 mark for writing a stanza about one of the given topics, 1 mark for using your answers to parts a) and b), 1 mark for using a regular rhyme scheme)*

Glossary

alliteration	When words that are close together start with the same sound. E.g. "a big blue bag".
audience	The person or group of people who listen to a text or watch a play.
context	The background to a text which affects the way the text is understood.
dialogue	A conversation between two or more people in a play or novel.
figurative language	Language that is used in a non-literal way to create an effect, e.g. personification.
hyperbole	When exaggeration is used to have an effect on the reader.
imagery	Language that creates a picture in your mind, e.g. metaphors and similes.
inference	Reaching an idea or conclusion, based on evidence.
list of three	Using three words (often adjectives) or phrases together to create emphasis.
metaphor	A way of describing something by saying that it is something else.
mood	The general feel or atmosphere of a text, e.g. humorous, peaceful, fearful.
narrative	Writing that tells a story or describes an experience.
narrator	The voice or character speaking the words of the narrative.
onomatopoeia	A word that imitates the sound it describes, e.g. "crunch".
personification	Describing a non-living thing as if it's a person. E.g. "The moon smiled at us."
purpose	The reason someone writes a text, e.g. to persuade, to argue, to advise, to inform.
rhetorical question	A question that doesn't need an answer but is asked to emphasise a point.
rhyming couplet	A pair of rhyming lines that are next to each other.
rhythm	A pattern of sounds created by the arrangement of syllables.
simile	A way of describing something by saying it is like something else.
stage directions	Written instructions in a play that describe how the play should be performed.
stanza	A group of lines in a poem, also known as a verse.
structure	The order and arrangement of ideas in a text. E.g. How it begins, develops and ends.
theme	A recurring idea in a play, novel or poem.
tone	The feeling created by the language of a piece of writing, e.g. happy, sad, serious.

Score Sheet

Fill in the score sheet after you finish each workout.

Write your scores below to show how you've done.
Each workout is out of 12 marks.

	Autumn Term	Spring Term	Summer Term
Workout 1			
Workout 2			
Workout 3			
Workout 4			
Workout 5			
Workout 6			
Workout 7			
Workout 8			
Workout 9			
Workout 10			
Workout 11			
Workout 12			